UTB

IN OTHER WORDS
SHEFFIELD UNITED'S PLAYERS

To
Lee
Merry Xmas 2018.

UTB!.!.

UTB

IN OTHER WORDS
SHEFFIELD UNITED'S PLAYERS

JOHN GARRETT

FOR MY WIFE, SARAH

First Published in Great Britain in 2018 by DB Publishing,
an imprint of JMD Media Ltd

ISBN 9781780915807

Printed and bound in the UK

CONTENTS

CHRIS WILDER

INTRODUCTION

I have known John Garrett for many years now – both as a player and now as the manager of Sheffield United Football Club – and it has to be said that John is never short of a word or two! Whatever role he has had at Bramall Lane, his love of the history of the Blades and the lads who have worn the shirt has brought him into contact with its history head on. He came up with the idea of Legends of the Lane, the Club Museum, and virtually single-handed built the fantastic collection of shirts, medals, Caps and other items that live their for fans to see – this research also put him into contact with the families of those long gone who had won them once again – the 'old boys' network just got bigger and bigger. This meant that, when a point of contact was needed for former players, he was the perfect choice

Most of the lads of my era knew John anyway, and the years he has been on the staff mean that all who follow have pretty much worked with him in his days as Player Liaison Officer – this means that he has plenty of contacts and phone numbers to go at, especially when it comes to needing an interview for the programme!

This collection gives a fascinating look at those who have gone before – there are a few of these legendary names that have now passed away – truly great names of the past – I was lucky to work side by side with Alan Hodgkinson during my time as manager of Oxford United. He is arguably one of our greatest ever keepers, and reading his piece brought back some fond memories of a truly great man and friend who is much missed.

I remember John phoning me one evening to do my piece and its incredible how life and football in particular can take you down some very strange roads indeed – I would never have dreamed back then that one day I would be Manager, and what a journey that was from being a Ball Boy, I can tell you!

The eras covered take you from pre-war right up to more or less modern day, and one of the many things that strike you is just how the game has changed in more ways than one. There are names such as Woodward that will be familiar to all, and names such as Widdowson that, possibly to a younger fan, will not be.

The common factor is that all lived the dream and pulled on a red and white shirt, and all played a part in the fantastic history that has built this Club, Sheffield United FC.

There are many stories – some happy, some sad, some laugh out funny and others that help you realise that, despite the hero worship you get from the terraces, football players are all human just like the rest of us. You also get a feeling of how proud we have all been to play for the Blades.

I hope you enjoy the book!

INTRODUCTION

The origins of this book go back to around 2012. I had already been writing my award-winning section 'Folklore and Fables' for a couple of seasons, and it seemed to go down really well – it still does. Our programme editor and close friend Kevin Cookson asked me if I fancied doing a piece each issue that involved talking to our former players about their life and times in the game. As I am a Former Player-Officer and have been in charge of the ex-player register for a number of years, it seemed to make perfect sense, and I agreed

Many of those who have played for the Club over the years I have worked for it are friends, and it is not hard to track down their whereabouts through the old boy's network if, for some reason, you have not got a number. One of my first jobs when the fixtures come out is to do the invites to return as guests up to Christmas, and I try to make it as different each season as I can. The lads bring a guest and either dine with TC in his suite on the John Street side from where they watch the game, or from the boardroom where they dine as guests of the owners.

All former players are always welcome to a couple of the best stand tickets I can lay my hands on for most games, and we have a fair few around all of the time. Many of them comment on how different we are as a Club. Curtis Woodhouse once told me that when he left for Birmingham City he thought that all clubs would be the same – players popping into the offices after training on a Friday for a brew, going for a swift half with the girls from the laundry on a day off, sleeping on a staff member's settee when they had been out to a presentation night and having Sunday dinner there the following day – a family. He will tell you the stark difference when he arrived at St Andrews – it just wasn't the same. We pride ourselves on being a family at Bramall Lane – it's as simple as that.

I was fortunate enough to interview one of the few surviving pre-war players at that time several times – the Blades legend that was Ephraim 'Jock' Dodds – at that point the oldest player to have appeared in an FA Cup Final who was still alive, and what a joy that was. Jock became a close and much-loved friend. Any journey to Blackpool for an audience with him was something to really look forward to. He was one hell of a character and never short of a tale about Sheffield United, his colleagues and football in general. He was invited, along with me, as guest of honor to the Arsenal v Chelsea FA Cup Final as I had written eight pages in the programme about our 1936 meeting with them at Wembley, which he had played in. Sadly, he was too ill to go at the time. That was a great pity as the old boy would have loved being walked round the pitch, taking in the applause from the fans. We did it here on the last game of the season v Burnley and it brought a lump to the throat as all four sides of Bramall Lane rose in appreciation of the last of his line. When he died, he left money in his will for me to 'buy a decent car and get rid of the dangerous crate that I was driving!'– I kid you not, that was the specific instruction and I had to provide the receipt. He was brilliant.

There are others who have, since interviewing, passed to a higher League. Alan Hodgkinson always had a aura around him, and you knew that when you were in his company you were in the presence of genuine Blades royalty. Fred Furniss was another who could talk of different times, the kind that it is hard to imagine these days; I mean, making your debut during an air raid? It was an honor to be asked by his family to speak at his funeral on behalf of Sheffield United and as a friend.

As I read back through the articles, I was so glad that every effort was made to bring Alan Woodward back to Sheffield for the 125th birthday celebrations in 2014. He was always genuinely bemused that fans still wanted to stop him in the car park for a talk and a selfie all those years after playing, quite often those who had never seen him kick a ball in anger for the Club. That's the thing with football, once a Club legend always a Club legend, and the three weeks he was here were fantastic fun. I think that he went back to Tulsa reluctantly on that occasion and the visit was made more poignant by his sudden passing the following year at home.

Who would have thought that, for instance, when I interviewed Chris Wilder, that he would lead the Blades out of the darkness and back into the Championship, holding the title trophy? He was always the man to do it as he proved at Oxford and Northampton. 'Hodgy' told me that and I would never have argued with him or doubted his judgement!

There are, of course, many different players featured, and I tried not to always go for the more obvious names. The stories of those who made fleeting appearances for the Club are often just as fascinating as the ones of those who racked up a few hundred. For every Chris Morgan there is an Ashley Fickling, and I believe that's how it should be in order to get a good balance.

I extend my thanks to every former player who has been kind enough to give their time for the content of this book over the years that the articles ran. None ever refused, some phoned me (on hands free) whilst travelling to talk, others put the kettle on and made me comfortable in their homes, others just popped in to work to have a chat

As a lifelong Blade, it is a truly great privilege to be in a position where I can do this. I have said before, one of the real joys of working for the Club is that heroes become friends, and interviewing them is both very easy and also a pleasure

I stopped doing the former-player section a couple of years ago to concentrate of writing 'Folklore and Fables', but, who knows, one day we may go with it again. There are still many that we haven't done – every season, as players depart and others join, there is more potential and more lives at the Lane to talk about. Every season creates new history, both good and bad. As they say, you never know.

John Garrett
November 2018

MARTIN PIKE

IN HIS DEFENCE

Quite by co-incidence, the day after the win over Fulham in the FA Cup, I caught up with former defender and Cottager's now former north-east scout Martin Pike, who talked about his fond memories of his time as a Blade during a period of change for the Club in the late 1980s, and of the lifelong friendships he forged during his time at the Lane – a time when the brief to manager Billy McEwan from the board was to go out and find young, hungry talent as cheaply as possible – a strategy that saw Pike join the Blades along with Peter Duffield, Peter Beagrie and a young Sheffield-born lad signed from Southampton by the name of Chris Wilder…

Billy McEwan was the manager who signed me from Peterborough United, although I was aware that United had been watching me for a while – in fact, it was Ian Porterfield in charge when I first got a heads up. I had joined Posh from West Brom; originally as a midfield player – in fact, I made my debut in that position and played quite a few games there.

John Wild was the manager then, and it was he that converted me to left back, and I enjoyed it. In fact, I got into the PFA Fourth Division team of the year as a result of my performances.

The deal with the Blades was on and off. One minute I was on the move, the next minute it fell through, and this happened a few times. I had all but given up when I was told to get the train up there to sort things out. I was met at Sheffield Midland by the smiling face of Danny Bergara, a great lad and a fine coach. He took me up to the Lane and I went into the Manager's office, where things were sorted out by Billy and Derek Dooley for the princely sum of £25,000.

Billy was trying to change things. There were still a few of the old guard around in the shape of John Burridge and Kevin Arnott, but he was trying to freshen things up. Peter Beagrie signed from 'Boro' the day after, and, to be

fair, 'Beags' was a great player – skilful with two great feet. We became and remain great friends – in fact we even bought houses on the same cul-de-sac in Beighton back then!

Another lifelong friendship was forged in the shape of Mark Todd. 'Toddy' had been there a little longer, but we hit it off straight away. I had broken up with my then girlfriend and needed a place to live in the short term. 'Toddy' lodged with a lady called Peggy Platt who had a house at Low Edges. Peggy was a Lane Legend – she had joined United in 1953 as laundry lady and when that got a bit much for her Derek Dooley had her making the tea and toast to make sure that she was still involved – it was a big part of her life and United were always a family club – they looked after their own.

She was like a mother to us both – brilliant, and I will never forget her kindness, bless her, it really cemented me with United and Sheffield. I still love the city and the feel it has. It's a special place and has a certain pull. I made my debut at Skegness Town in a pre-season friendly and felt like I belonged. It was a big Club and I was proud to pull on that famous shirt.

Tony Philliskirk was around then – he was from the same area of the North East as I was – we had played football against each other as kids – so was Clive Mendonca. Happy days! My first season was ok; we finished ninth in the old Division Two and I played in pretty well every game. The difference between the Fourth and Second [Division] was vast, but I think that I adapted really well. I can honestly say that I really enjoyed it. The following season was a different one altogether, we struggled badly and, after being on the wrong end of a 5-0 battering at Bramall Lane on 2nd January v Oldham Athletic, McEwan was sacked. Danny took over in the interim.

His replacement was, of course, Dave Bassett (nicknamed 'Harry'). That was the time when there was a play off to see who got relegated. I had missed a run of games with an injured toe in the lead up. The opponents were Bristol City. We lost 1-0 down there – Carl Shutt, a Sheffield lad who had played for Wednesday, scored and took a fair bit of grief from our fans – we drew the home leg 1-1 and that was that, we were down.

'Harry' was great – we began to really take some shape and he brought some great players in like Tony Agana and Brian Deane – the dressing room and the atmosphere just got better and better. The best game I ever played in was in the FA Cup v Norwich City – I really mean that. We lost 3-2, but our fans were magnificent at Carrow Road that day, and the Canaries had a top-class side that were always there or thereabouts back then – Andy Townsend and players of that calibre.

I had managed to break my duck in terms of scoring that season. The first came against Blackpool away – over my career I had a great record against them – I also got a brace against Notts County on Boxing Day 1989. Brian Deane got sent off in that match! 'Harry' worked well on set pieces and we really benefitted from that – I also scored one straight from a corner, so there's not only Alan Woodward who was capable of that!

IN OTHER WORDS

That was my last full season as a Blade – we got promoted and it was brilliant to have played a part. Over the summer the gaffer brought Dave Barnes in. We went on the pre-season tour and I had struggled to play – an insect bite on my toe had caused problems. I was desperate to play and ended up getting sent off. The season began, and I played and all looked well. The ref, however, had gone away for a holiday and then decided to submit the red card when he came back. All of a sudden Geoff Taylor took me to one side and told me that they had found out the suspension had to stand – I was gutted. 'Barnsey' got in and played well. Harry was always loyal to players when they were doing well and that was pretty much it for me – that was followed by Wilf Rostron, so I was well down the order.

I needed to play football and they let me go out on loan, first to Tranmere. I enjoyed it, but bad weather meant that appearances were restricted there. The next was to Bolton Wanderers. We played six, won four and drew two, and I loved it. Phil Neal was manager and I did all I could to get a move there. Tony Philiskirk was also there and I was traveling over from Sheffield with former Owl David Reeves. Once again, it just didn't happen. My last game was v Fulham, and Jeff Eckhardt, who I knew from Bramall Lane, told me that they had been keeping tabs. After returning to the Lane a deal was done and Ray Lewington signed me [for Fulham].

That started a relationship that lasts to this day. I am their scout in the North East and am always on the lookout for the next rough diamond to be polished. I loved United and I love Sheffield – it's great to get back to the Lane now and watch games, which I do quite a few times a season. There are always familiar faces in the stands that make me really welcome and staff like Mick Rooker and Johnny Garrett who I have known for years.

I hope the Blades kick on under Chris and get back to where they deserve to be. It's a great club – a special club

FOOTNOTE

At the time of the interview Martin was still the northern scout for Fulham, a Club he had served for many years, also as a player, and one that the fans had the highest regard for. As often happens in football, a change of ownership and manager brought different ideas and staff, and as a result the two parties parted company, much to his obvious disappointment. Following him joining us as a guest for a game, he turned up at the staff Christmas party in the company of long-time friend and then Northampton Town manager Chris Wilder to celebrate the festive season with Blades friends of old – who would have thought at that point that Chris would soon be manager of the Blades?

'Pikey' is still working in football, but now performing the same role up here for Chelsea, so maybe all's well that ends well there.

LEE MORRIS

SON OF GOD?

There have been a few notable father-and-son Blades down the years. I caught up with half of one in the shape of Lee Morris, son of 80s legend Colin, who, it has to be said, is one of my all-time Blades heroes. Lee put his side of the story of his time at Bramall Lane as well as the aborted return at the end of his time at Derby County…

I was actually born in Blackpool but came to Sheffield when Dad signed for the Blades, and I would be about two, so my earliest memories are that of Sheffield United FC and the Steel City, and I love the place. It is still very much a feel of going home when I come back there.

Dad went to Scarborough and we moved to a little village near to Driffield, where I went to school – that where I first came across Curtis Woodhouse – we became good friends and still are today. We turned out for a local team, Bridlington Rangers – Richard Cresswell was a couple of years above us there. Later on we all appeared in the same England side; that must be quite rare to have a junior club produce Three Lions from one side! There is a great picture of us all together and kitted up that I love – it was in the local papers and, I think, the Sheffield United programme of the time.

It was York City who first took notice of us and we went there, where the coach was the excellent Ricky Sbragia – he was superb, but there was always going to be a pull between the Morris clan and Bramall Lane. Dad was still very much in touch with the Blades and there was no contest when I knew that they wanted me – Curtis came as well.

I was 12 and you couldn't sign back then until 14. I came across to the training camps in the holidays, and then put pen to paper as an apprentice aged 16. I couldn't wait to get there, it was, and is, my Club and I am proud that Dad is held in such esteem with the fans to this day. I lodged on Psalter Lane with Anne and she was brilliant – thankfully Curtis was with a few others like

'Stricks' [Rob Strickland] at Rita's on Abbeydale Road, and I was so glad mine was a happy and peaceful existence and theirs was the kind of carnage that tends to go hand in hand with Curt! If I wanted to go and have a laugh I did, but I could go back to sanity if and when I wanted – brilliant!

Dave Bassett was manager when I got there, and then Howard Kendall, but it would be Nigel Spackman who gave me my shot at the big time. I well remember travelling down to the Play-off Final v Crystal Palace with the other apprentices and the late David Hopkin goal was like a knife through the heart of the Club – that said, I am sure had we gone back up the younger players like me would have had less of a chance – it's funny how things work out.

I remember being ball boys – Curtis and me were on the John Street side as it was being rebuilt when we played Man City – it was a building site still, and if the ball went out across the work area, the later in the game it got, Curtis was taking longer and longer to get it back – I think he even stopped and tried to tie his laces at one point! The City players and fans were going mad! It was so funny and Don Hutchinson high-fived him at the end – we won 2-0!

My first-team debut came as a sub v Wolves and my start in a shirt away at Crewe in January 1999, even though I had been on the bench a fair few times under Nigel Spackman and then Steve Thompson. I remember coming on as sub against Coventry in the replay at Bramall Lane when 'Quinny' scored the pen that took us through to the Semi-Final in front of the Kop – what a night that was. The fans mobbed the pitch and back then I had the same haircut as he did, so people thought that I was him and proceeded to carry me around the pitch on their shoulders – who was I to tell them I wasn't 'Quinny', it was great!

I should have been involved in the Semi-Final against Newcastle at Old Trafford, but I was suspended; I had played for the Under-21s against Leeds and they had kicked me from pillar to post – I had stud marks from my arse to my ankle, I can tell you! I told the ref he was a cheat and not giving anything our way, and he took exception to my opinion – I was off and no FA Cup Semi. Devastated!

I also bagged one in the abandoned game away at Arsenal when the goal was scored against us through unsporting conduct – Arsene Wenger offered a replay and we went back down there. We lost again, and I also managed to score in that one – Steve Bruce wanted to take us off the pitch in protest in the first game, but Graham Stuart was sensible enough to keep one foot on the Highbury Turf, otherwise we would have been in trouble for leaving the field of play!

I ruptured my fifth metatarsal whilst with England Under-18s, and that was the time before David Beckham made it trendy and I was out for nearly a year – even at that age it was a long and hard road back and there were many times that I thought that was that. It helped me later as I have managed to do that on three occasions!

I wasn't aware that the Club wanted to sell me; I hadn't played a first-team game in an age, trained on Thursday, came on as sub at Crewe on the Saturday and was on my way to Derby the next week - the Club wanted a deal and it was for about £3 million – not bad bucks back then.

I loved Derby, but as my contract was coming to a close the Blades expressed an interest in bringing me home – it was a no brainer, all I wanted to do was be back at Bramall Lane. United were second and Norwich were top, and all was cleared for me to have a medical in Sheffield the day the Rams and Blades played each other at Pride Park. I passed that fine and the manager had agreed to leave me out of the squad. I got there late and missed the first half.

The Blades played Norwich on the Saturday and I was supposed to sign on the Sunday. I rang the Club to find out when and where – I rang loads of times but didn't get a call back – this went on for a few days. This was the season of the first transfer window, and I still got no reply. Leicester got wind and offered me the same deal. After giving up with coming home, I signed, and then certain people went to the press and said that I had gone back on my word. It wasn't the case; I had done all I could. It hurt like hell when I came back as a sub with the Foxes and got booed. The Blades were my Club and I was one of them – just wanted to set the record straight there!

I worked with Nigel Clough, Andy Garner, Gary Crosby and Matt Brown at Burton Albion, and all I can say is how lucky United are to have them at the Lane. Nigel is a top bloke, a real person, and I cannot speak highly enough of him. It's always the first result I look for and I am a coach at Derby's Academy thanks to him.

IN OTHER WORDS

I am also manager of Loughborough Dynamo and last week we played a League game away at Goole Town where, of course, the manger is my old mate Curtis Woodhouse! It was a 0-0 draw and, as always, we put the world to rights after the game. We go back a long way and we both love Sheffield United – simple as that really.

FOOTNOTE

It is so sad that if you look at the obvious talent Lee had and the Clubs that he played for over the years of his career, injury restricted him to around 150 appearances in the League, nowhere near what his obvious talent merited. I remember how hard he worked to get into the United side as youngster – a fact that, I suspect, wasn't made any easier by his Dad being a Lane legend in the shape of Colin. Since the interview Lee has found himself working as a football coach out in America, and the last time I spoke with him he was loving life over there and enjoying giving something back to the game as a coach now and not a player. In his time at the Club, along with Curtis Woodhouse and Wayne Quinn, who was a little older and got his break before the others, they were nicknamed 'The Spice Boys'. They were the first crop we had seen through the ranks really since Mitch Ward had followed Dane Whitehouse and the Smith brothers, and they were young and stood out from the rest. Lee is a cracking lad who has never forgotten that the Blades gave him his chance.

JOHN GANNON

CUT-PRICE QUALITY

A Dave Bassett signing that, all these years on, is still an honorary Sheffielder living in the city, Gannon was a typical 'Harry' signing – he cost next to nothing and went on to spend seven years at Bramall Lane, making 196 (13) appearances. He took time to settle and win over the crowd, but all who saw him realised what a pivotal part of the team he became, as a master of the set piece and dead ball – John took up his story for the programme back in 2015...

The first time I came up to Bramall Lane was as a youngster with Wimbledon. I was an apprentice and we were battling for promotion. The game was at the back end of the season and the Blades won by two goals to one. All ended well for both – the Dons went up and United did the same at the end of the season. The game had an incredible atmosphere. Much has been written about Plough Lane, but Bramall Lane was completely different – a big ground

and a Club with a great heritage. There were over 22,000 there that day and the atmosphere was incredible, and it left a hell of an impression.

Dave Bassett had been a big influence on me. I still speak with 'Harry' today, so when he came in for me it was the chance for a new challenge. Sheffield United were shopping in the bargain basement of football and 'Harry' was a man who could find a bargain and no mistake there. It was made easier for a Southerner as there were a fair few more up there already, and more than a fair smattering of Wimbledon lads. Simon Tracey had signed about six months before and he was a good friend, so I moved in with him at South Anston and loved it. Brian Deane and Ian Bryson lived on the same road, so it was a good place to be.

I came into a promotion season late, and we were in fantastic form, there was no doubt about that. Tony and 'Deano' were unstoppable, but you don't need me to tell you that. We had a team that knew how to dig in and win games – no matter what, we always felt that we had goals in us and proved it time and time again. Of course, we went up that year into what was the old Division Two.

Back-to-back promotion is something very special, and I am proud to think that I played my part for the Club there – that second season when we were neck-and-neck with Leeds United right up to the wire was something else. The Bramall Lane crowd can be a hard one, because the people in S2 know their football. I know that I wasn't always everyone's cup of tea and the expectations can be very high at Bramall Lane, and quite rightly so. The stick I got helped me grow up a lot as a player and very quickly indeed.

I broke my arm against Port Vale towards the end of the campaign that saw us regain our top-flight status. It was really hard to watch from the sidelines with my arm in a sling, but I was in good company – we had a few real injury worries towards the end and skipper Paul Stancliffe watched with me at Leicester in what was a hell of a game – 5-2, and we had done it – fairytale stuff. And we knew that it would be a titanic achievement to keep the Club in the top flight of the English game, but keep them there we did, and for a good couple of years.

I never hid, I never would, and would like to think that the fans recognized this. I supplied a lot from set plays – think of the double over our neighbours. When we played them at Bramall Lane it was the first time we had come across them in the League for a long time – nearly 15 years – and the talk was all about the footballing masterclass that they were about to serve us up on a platter.

As history shows, the reality was very different. In a white-hot game, we won by two goals to nil and I played a part in both of those goals on a day that I will never forget. It was the same over at their place – I crossed the ball in for what, if I remember correctly, was Bobby Davison's second goal to see the Leppings Lane end erupt. Priceless stuff.

It was funny that, despite my regard and respect for Harry, it was sad when Dave Bassett left, but he was replaced by Howard Kendall. I think I played some of the best football of my career under him. When he came in, a lot of the old guard feared for their shirt, but for a time all went well for me. When I eventually left Sheffield United I was sad – I had and still have a massive affinity with the Blades – I may have been a youngster at Wimbledon, but I grew up at Sheffield United, there is no doubt about that.

I still keep in regular contact with many of my teammates, such as Trace. We were a strong unit and the bond still holds all these years on.

Financially, after a tough couple of years, the Club was beginning to recover, and it would have been nice to have played another part in things, but that is football; when it's time to go then it's time to go, and with my contract being up the chance to go to Oldham Athletic presented itself and away I went.

Sheffield is still my home today, and I try and watch us as much as possible, although I still work in the game for Manchester City. I know what our fans are like and the passion and noise they can display at Wembley; I was fortunate to be a part of one of our games down there, so I hope with all my heart that it can be the Blades who walk out there this season in one of the Semi-Finals of the FA Cup – if that's the case I will be on the terraces cheering us on, of that I can assure you.

FOOTNOTE

Over 20 years after making his last appearance for United, John is yet another former player who joined The Blades, loved the City and the Blades and, as a result, stayed and built a family and life in South Yorkshire.

Who would have thought that the bargain buy from Wimbledon would end up as European scout for arguably the most powerful club currently in the English Premier League? It's clear that the knowledge his many years in the game have built is greatly valued over the Pennines, and for good reason.

I was always a huge fan of him as a player – all sides need a John Gannon – the heartbeat that makes a team tick like a well-oiled watch – and that's just what he did for us so well.

He did it without fuss or palaver, just went out there and got on with things in his own way and that takes class.

BOB BOOKER

OOH ARR WHAT A STAR!

Playing for the Blades always seems to stay with those who have pulled on the famous shirt long after they have left, and Bob Booker is, without a doubt, one of those regarded by anyone who saw him play as a real Legend of the Lane — maybe not for his silky skills but for his attitude and commitment to the cause. He never hid and gave his all for Sheffield United and that formed a unique bond between the man and the fans. Bob tells his story…

I left school at a young age and took an apprenticeship as an upholsterer, and played for our local team – I was up front with one Derek French who would one day play a big part in my Sheffield United story. A young Vinnie Jones was also in our midfield.

I came to Brentford's attention and got a trial. I must have done OK as they offered me a contract and it was a big opportunity, a football player was all I had ever wanted to be. As an upholsterer I was on 200 quid a week back then – I did piece work and sometimes it could be as much as £300, big money in the late 1970s. Brentford was £60, but well worth the gamble, and I did well down the years I was there.

In '86 I did my cruciate ligament and it took me nearly two years to come back, but I was determined to recover and I got there in the end. Sheffield United were in our division and they came to Griffin Park – I recall they filled the upper and lower of the KLM stand and the noise was unbelievable. I had a mare and Steve Perryman took me off with about 20 minutes to go – the Blades won.

I travelled home with Frenchy – we lived near each other and he was now, of course, physio of Bramall Lane. I couldn't get over United, they had a great team with Brian Deane and Tony Agana banging them in, and I said to Derek that it must be brilliant to be part of something like that. I got a phone call early the following week from Frenchy who told me that Dave Bassett was interested in signing me; he had tried before when he was at Wimbledon, but nothing ever

came of it. Simon Webster had been badly injured, and he needed some legs – I went to see Steve Perryman, who was great – I wasn't in his plans and as far as he was concerned I was welcome to go on a free if I could get sorted out.

I went up to Sheffield with my Dad the following day in my battered old Ford Fiesta, and I well recall pulling into the Cherry Street car park to be confronted by the frontage of the South Stand. Before I had even had talks I had signed in my head already! We sat and talked to Dave Bassett and Derek Dooley – what a great man Derek was, God bless him, one of the very best.

He went through what they would pay me, signing on, bonus, where I would live etc. and I just sat stunned – this was a different ballgame. I was, at the age of 32, looking at the end of my career and here was a Club of this size and stature offering me what I considered was the world. Derek said, 'there you go son – maybe you and your Dad would like to step outside and have a talk about things?' In those days Dad was my advisor – no flashy over-paid agents.

It was the classic *Only Fools and Horses* moment. We stood in the corridor and looked at each other, 'do you want to go first?' he asked. We both danced round together laughing – this was all a fairytale and they must have heard us in DD's room. We went back in and I signed – it was the best thing I have ever done.

I came back up the following day and played in the reserves at Huddersfield – I then made my debut at the weekend against Bristol City. It would be fair to say that I found it hard to settle at the beginning. Brentford tended to play very neat tippy-tappy football and I was used to receiving the ball – passing it – creating space. We played to the strengths of the players – physically very fit, but the ball was worked up to 'Deano' and Tony very quickly and it was effective.

I was knackered running down the field to pick the ball up from, say, Martin Pike, and arrived there to see it go flying over my head – I spent that much time to-ing and fro-ing that when I got the ball I was that knackered and I didn't know what to do with it!

Mick Rooker, the Promotions Manager at Sheffield United, gave me the best advice ever. We became lifelong friends when I signed, and we would go out for a beer – one night over a pint he told me to slow down and not to hide. If the Bramall Lane crowd thinks you are being flash and having a bad game they will kill you – if they can see that you aren't frightened and will put you in 100 per cent without hiding they will get behind you. It was wise advice – I did what he suggested and the rest, as they say, is history.

It all changed at Mansfield Town on a miserable rainy night. Our fans were brilliant – we won 2-0 and 'Oooh Aaah Bob Bookah' was born – I was always so proud when they sang it – still am. I remember when I Captained the team at Leicester in the promotion clincher and what a day that was – I was in a decent challenge with Gary McAllister and laid out on the floor. He leaned over me and asked, 'Who the f--- are you?' As he did it the crowd were chanting my name. 'I'm Ooh aah Bob Bookah pal – listen.' He was bemused to say the least!

IN OTHER WORDS

I love Sheffield United and Sheffield as a city. I lived firstly in the same house as Geoff Taylor, the Assistant Manager, and Jock Bryson in Nether Edge, and it drove me mad – Bryson's snoring was terrible! I then moved in with Chris Wilder and Tony Agana at Gleadless – Tony had that saxophone that you saw in the United documentary – the only trouble was that he only knew one bloody song!!! I finished up at Martin Pike's house on Mitchell Road at Woodseats along with my rottweiller dog Bruno – and we had many a night in the Big Tree – happy days!

I have so many magic memories: the goal at QPR that kept us up – Andy Daykin told me that I saved the Club a million pounds – still waiting for the bonus though! – Leicester, as I have said, the first game v Liverpool – all chances that I thought had gone past me. Derek Dooley gave me a new contract when the first came up for renewal, and I just signed it – why wouldn't I? After dinner I went back to see him. As I stuck my head round the door of his office he said, 'no chance Bob – there's no more money son, that's it.' I told him that I just wanted to thank him again for giving me a new deal and tell him that I would never let him or the Club down. He said in his biography that it was the first time a player had ever done that and it brought a tear to his eye – Derek was a top, top man, one of the very best in the game and I thought the world of him.

When the time came for me to leave, I was gutted, but knew that the timing was right. Sheffield United gave me some of the very best memories of my time in football, and they still remain bright today. One night we were having dinner with some friends at my house in Watford when we all heard some drunken singing outside at the bottom of the drive. When I went out to investigate, I found a load of Blades lads on their way back from an away game who had tracked me down and just wanted to sing my name! i invited them all up to the house for a beer! I thought it was brilliant, but I'm not too sure what the then missus and the other guests thought about it! I worked for many years on the coaching staff at Brighton – I still do match day hosting for them to this day, and I, loved every minute of that, but the Sheffield United pull never leaves. When Mickey Adams was manager it was fantastic – he is a life long Blade as many know, so we always had an affinity. I get back to Sheffield as much as I can- I now run a driving school and, as I said, work for the Seagulls at weekends, but Bramall Lane will never be far from my heart.

LEN BADGER

RED, WHITE AND BLACK WITH TWO ON HIS BACK

Anyone of an age will tell you how good a player Len Badger was. A Sheffield lad who worked hard to get his chance at United, it could be said that his loyalty to the red and white probably cost him major International honours. One of the true characters of the Club, we are fortunate to see Len on a regular basis as he hosts sponsors on the day of a game. A few pages can never do him justice as he has plenty to tell you, some unprintable but always funny! Take it away Len...

I was born and bred in Sheffield – Darnall to be precise – in 1945 (there is no truth that Hitler surrendered as a result!) and some of my earliest memories of football were kicking around on an area of land down there that all of the kids knew as 'Little Wembley' – there were some fair old games and battles fought on there, I can tell you!

IN OTHER WORDS

I was a pupil at Coleridge Road School and I played for them at inside right – I was considered good enough to play for Sheffield Boys, but they decided that I would be a right back, so it all started there I suppose. I remember playing for them against Nottinghamshire Boys and in their team at that time was Mick Jones and Alan Birchenall, both of whom would feature in my life quite prominently – there was also a young David Pleat. He was a lovely player but a bit of a lightweight and didn't make it as a pro, although he wasn't a bad manager in his day!

My Dad died when I was fairly young, but when he took me to games it was always at Bramall Lane and there was only ever one club and that was, and indeed still is, Sheffield United FC. I have always been a Blade and I am truly proud of that – it means everything.

Things were not easy and there was not a lot of money around – Hilda, my Mum, did a magnificent job of bringing me up and making sure I was OK, and although things were tight I had a very happy upbringing in a part of Sheffield that really was a big village – you always read the tales of people saying that you could leave your door open night and day without owt going missing, and in Darnall that was true back then.

I joined United as a youngster and made my way up through the ranks before I was lucky enough to become an apprentice. I actually signed in August 1962 and John Harris was the manager who gave me my chance. John was fantastic with both me and Mum, but more of that later on. I was lucky enough to play for England, first as a schoolboy, then as a youth – in fact, I represented England at every level bar a full cap – many said that was because I played for what was considered an 'unfashionable' club in the shape of Sheffield United. If that was the case, then so be it – I only ever wanted to play in the red and white stripes and that was all that mattered, and I would take that over an England cap any time! It's a good job really, isn't it?! That said, I was around and in Alf Ramsay's World Cup Shadow Squad in 1966, so I am proud that I got that far – I mean, there were some good players weren't there? They won the World Cup!

Life as a youngster at Bramall Lane was never dull and we were always up to no good – a favorite initiation for new youngsters was to cram them in to one of the wicker kit baskets, tie it up and shove them in the showers with cold water cascading in and filling up. This went well until one day we forgot about a victim and very nearly drowned him! Needless to say, we eased off then. Others have been hung upside down from the floodlights, swaying gracefully in the wind! There used to be loads of service tunnels that honeycombed under the John Street stand – pitch black, dirty and dusty. For a dare I went exploring one day after training. After a fair time, I realised that I was lost – couldn't see a thing, could I? On I crawled, and by this time I was getting more and more worried. Suddenly I saw a thin chink of light and made for it in the confined space. I pushed, and it gave a bit – once again I got my full shoulder behind it and it gave with a crack – it was a trap door and it was flung back to reveal my manager John Harris with chairman Dick Wragg in conversation in his office!

John Harris didn't swear ever, but he shouted, 'Len, what the blimmin' heck is going on?' Believe me, that was strong for the boss, and I was in trouble again. I got into plenty of scrapes, but he would always let me off. That got me the nickname of 'son of' with a few of the lads!

I made my first-team bow whilst on the tour of the USA and Canada, and it came as a sub against St Louis All Stars on 23rd May 1962, and got my first start a week later. The tours we undertook in those days were legendary. John Harris was a tee-total Methodist who never married, apart from to football, and that meant when the season ended he had nothing to do, so we all got dragged off on some amazing tours. What an experience for a young lad from Sheffield, and there were a few of us in the squad back then. Hettie Shaw (Joe's wife) has some cine film of some of the excursions as Joe always took a camera with him, and they have been put to DVD, what great memories they stir up some 50 years on.

I came into a team that was full of Blades Legends, and I made my League debut on 26th April 1963 at Bramall Lane against Leyton Orient. I had played in the League Cup away at Bury the previous October. I took the shirt of one of our greats in the shape of Cec Coldwell. Cec was one of our greatest servants, who would also go on to be an important member of the coaching staff and have two spells as Caretaker-Manager – great player and a great man.

Also in the team that day were Alan Hodgkinson, Doc Pace, Joe Shaw, Graham Shaw, Gerry Summers and Brian Richardson. Doc Pace was one of our most prolific strikers ever, and the defence wrote itself into Blades folklore with me sitting in it. I did so well it was my last first-team shout that term!

The following season I got a few more starts, but it was 1964/65 when I made the position my own. I saw Alan Birchenall say in the programme last season that Harris was brave by replacing the old guard very quickly with the superb youth they had, and I have to agree. I am proud of many things, but the fact that I am still the youngest-ever league Captain in our great club's history is the one I will never top, and I was handed the armband by Joe Shaw. We all called him 'Father', a term of endearment at Sheffield United for a senior player – I know Joe called Albert Cox the same thing a generation before. He was like a dad to me – he and his wife were so good to me, really kind, and I will never forget that.

I have played with some fine players, but the side that was assembled for promotion in 1971 was one of the best: 'TC', 'Big Eddie', 'Bill', 'Hems', the list goes on. We were entertainers and played football on the floor – capable of winning 5-0 one week and losing 6-2 the next – it was never dull! As one of the players, I was also a fan. I recall playing away in Algeria and seeing 'Shred' – a proper Blade was 'Shred' – he was behind the net and there were only a couple of them – I let them kip in our hotel room, I mean, we are all part of the same thing, aren't we? One of the other players objected and I pointed out that he should mind his own business, he wasn't one of us so what did he know?

I was honoured to have a testimonial game at Bramall Lane in 1973. In fact, I had a great testimonial season. To promote the events, I drove round in an old Austin Cambridge painted red and white with number two on it. This worked ok until I got pulled over at Meadowhead by the Police and done for it being unroadworthy! Thanks for that! Hemsley was in the passenger seat and hid behind a copy of the *Racing Post* while I was getting my collar felt.

Jimmy Sirrell sold me to Chesterfield – I didn't want to go! But it was a nice club and I enjoyed it there until injury finished my career – after that I moved into business and I have had a few successful pubs that were frequented by Blades down the years – the last one being the Fox and Goose at Wigley, from where I retired a couple of years ago.

I have some great memories and keep in touch with many of the lads – the '71 team of course – Hemsley is like a brother, as is TC and all to be honest.

Ken Mallender and Colin Addison are still close and I speak to Denis Shiels still as well – another proper lad.

I am at pretty well every home game and occasionally the odd away. I love Sheffield United – its stadium, its fans, its history and culture. After the game, even though I will have been in the Platinum Suite hosting, I like nothing better than having a glass in the Railway and chatting with our fans, because that it what I am and have always been – the difference is that I was one of the ones lucky enough to have had the chance to pull on the stripes. 541 appearances – not bad for a Darnall lad, is it?!

FOOTNOTE

If you chopped his head off, he would bleed red and white (and maybe a drop or two of red wine!). Our youngest-ever league Captain only ever wanted to play for one club, and that loyalty probably cost him dearly in the game. He tells me that he never earned more than a basic wage of £75 per week in a first-team career that lasted nearly 15 years, and I believe him.

The phrase 'proper lad' is used in the interview, and there couldn't be a better description of Sir Len. Hysterically funny, when meeting lifelong friend Ted Hemsley on the day he signed from Shrewsbury Town, he introduced himself as 'Head of Entertainments for the Football Club', and that is probably a very fair description!

Although he will become embarrassed when you tell him, Len Badger is also one of the greatest full backs ever to represent Sheffield United FC. Cultured and gifted, he should have had a bag full of England Caps at full level and not just the junior levels and Football League call-ups that he got. They talk about national treasures, well Len Badger is a Sheffield United treasure, of that, there is no doubt.

FRED FURNISS

PENALTY KING

I have been fortunate to have met many famous Blades – when I started working for the Club there were still a few of the real old boys around, and one of the nicest of them all was Fred Furniss. Still reasonably active when the piece was written in 2015, Fred was one of the last who had seen footballing action before the end of World War Two. League Championship winner, county-standard crown green bowler and formidable on the green baize, Fred was, without a doubt, a truly great character.

I am a Sheffield lad and very proud of the fact. I was born in 1922 and as a youngster I went to Phillimore Road School in Darnall – that was a very different area back then – a lot of industry and back-to-back housing, but it was a real community spirit in those days. I liked sport and was decent at many different things, but it was football that I really loved. I did very well and was lucky enough to play for both Sheffield and Yorkshire boys. Harold Brook did as well. 'Brooky' would play with me in the same Sheffield United team and he was a good 'un – he never gets the credit he deserves – a clever player who served United very well and Captained them to promotion in 1953 before the Club were daft enough to let him go to Leeds United.

I originally signed for the Club as an amateur – you don't get those nowadays – and we trained at Bramall Lane on a Tuesday and Thursday evening. The manager was Teddy Davison and he was, I think, the first proper manager in the modern sense. He also had quite an eye for a player. As I signed, the war was in its fairly early stages and United had been at the top of the old First Division when the League was abandoned after they had been promoted the previous season.

The war got in the way of a lot of careers. Ernest Jackson was as good a player in defence as you could wish to see, and he lost his best years. Jimmy Hagan was the same, although Jim was class and still as good as you could

get when the war had ended, one of the greatest ever to play for Sheffield United FC. The war gave a chance to a lot of younger players, and I made my debut away at Goodison Park against Everton, and I doubt that you could have made your debut in more bizarre circumstances. An air raid happened, and we played on with sirens wailing in the background and the ack ack guns blasting away. Hitler tried to stop the Blades winning and nearly succeeded – we ended up drawing 3-3 and I did fairly well as I remember back then.

Don't forget, the war years were not 'Football League' as the programme had been abandoned, so I didn't really make my league debut until 1946. I carried on through the war and I also worked for a Sheffield company called Hamptons for a while before a became a Bevan boy – that was working down the coal mines and there were a lot of lads that went doing that. I was down Orgreave near Handsworth, where the famous battle would take place many years later during the miners' strike. I didn't mind it and was never afraid of hard work, but I had the wits scared out of me when I was nearly hit by a huge coal tub that they used for moving the stuff from the coal face. That made my mind up that I was better in the army than underground and I joined the Royal Artillery.

As I said, I still got chances to play and I became a regular in the side in late 1943, and I kept my place until I finished in 1954 – not bad really. I think I was a decent player, but I always tried to be consistent without letting people down and I played at right back, although at times I would also describe myself as what we would call a wing half in old money, and I used to like to get up and give the forwards some support. We had some cracking lads and I was really proud when we won the Wartime Division One North Championship and also being a part of the first team to play in Berlin after the surrender at the Olympic Stadium against a Forces XI. That was a caper, we flew out from a Lincolnshire air base on a military aircraft – I have never been as scared! You could see the floor through gaps between the boards as we took off!

I was also a decent penalty taker – you would have to check this, but I believe over my career I took 17 and I only missed a couple – not bad! I was also lucky that I played a part in the 1952/53 Championship side at the back end of my career, and the medal is one of my prized possessions, along with the County Cup ones that I was lucky to get in my time – great times and great memories.

My last game as a Blade came in a defeat to Sheffield Wednesday before I went and had a time at Chesterfield – Teddy Davison had gone back there when he was replaced by Reg Freeman and then Joe Mercer at Bramall Lane, and the Club even got a £400 transfer fee for me after all that service!

When I had finished as a professional football player, I had a business in Sheffield, but always carried on playing in the old Leagues like the Hatchard in local football – I was still giving people a game in my mid-50s! I looked after myself and still enjoyed myself, so why not? I also refereed many a Sunday League match for youngsters – I had been lucky with the breaks I got so it was right and good to give a bit back.

I did a bit of scouting as well – one of the lads I saw as a ref I recommended to Chesterfield, who I was keeping an eye out for, and he did quite well – his name was Gordon Banks and he picked a World Cup-Winner's medal up in 1966 – not bad for a lad from Tinsley, and United could have had him – they thought he was too small!

I was a decent snooker player, and when I could get around a bit better I was a fair crown green bowler – I loved that.

I think I am also the only player to read his own obituary! The *Sheffield Star* ran a story that I had died; there were some lovely tributes to me. I never realised how popular I was! There were a lot of surprised faces that afternoon when I turned up to play, I think one or two may have fainted with shock. I didn't look bad for a corpse! Robert Jackson of Radio Sheffield fame used to bowl with me – lovely man is Robert – the man who invented 'Praise or Grumble' – no one was more shocked to see me then him!

I don't get to that many games now age has caught up with me. I live with my daughter and she brings me to Senior Blades events and I enjoy it very much. I loved my time as a football player, met some wonderful people and have enjoyed a great life – I still am!

FOOTNOTE

Fred passed to a higher League in May 2017, and I was honoured to be asked by his daughter to speak on behalf of the Club at his funeral. I loved him to bits – up till not too long before the end he could tell you stories of games and players long gone – a different time for the Club and society in general, and an incredible barometer of change. These days, we are delighted if we produce a player every couple of years who has what it takes to get into the first team and sustain it – back then, there was an old saying that all you had to do, if you wanted to find a footballer or cricketer, was go to the top of a mine shaft and shout!

Look at League Championship-winning side that Fred played in, in 1952/53 – he came from Sheffield, Harold Brook came from Sheffield, Graham Shaw came from Sheffield, Harry Latham did and so did Joe Shaw – that's not forgetting others such as Cec Coldwell and Arthur Bottom who were getting closer to being regulars. Joe Shaw was from just up the road outside Doncaster in Upton (despite being born in the North East) and keeper Ted Burgin also heralded from the Steel City as well – incredible!

I used to sort out his match tickets – he never wanted the fuss of corporate, just to sit side by side with other fans enjoying the game. I often wonder if anyone re-alised what a legend the little old man was sitting next to them in the South Stand. He was always down at the ground early, firstly to pick up his ticket and secondly to sit on the wall outside, enjoying the build up and people arriving. If I spotted

him I would always take him along on the sponsor tour, and many times ended up losing him, only to backtrack and find him sat there as the lads got changed, nattering away to Chris Morgan about the game. When I told them who he was and what he had done for the Club, they were astonished!

Fred lived to a ripe old age and remains the only Blades player I can think of to have lived to read his own obituary – he thought it was hilarious and didn't take it to heart – he told me he was grateful it wasn't his and that was that.

A great character and great player, the likes of which became extinct in the game a long, long time ago.

PAUL STANCLIFFE

LOCAL HERO

When you talk about players who the fans regard with complete respect, one of the first names out the hat is always that of Paul Stancliffe, and quite rightly so. 'Stan' is in charge of the Under-21s at our neighbours, Doncaster Rovers, so not a million miles away from his spiritual roots. This interview was done in 2013, but little has changed, he is still with Donny at the Keepmoat and still in love with the game...

I am a born-and-bred Sheffield lad; in fact, I was born not too far away from Bramall Lane on Hanover Square near to the church that is still there to this day. In fact, my mum and dad got married there. I lived in the area for a couple of years before we moved up to Parson Cross; Colley to be precise

Now, you would think that I would have been a Blade, spending my early years so near to the ground, but my Dad was Wednesday and as a kid I used to go to Hillsborough with him on a fairly regular basis. I was playing for my school when Danny Williams, the Wednesday manager, spotted me and I was invited to train with them – in fact, it was a figure familiar to many Blades in the shape of George McCabe who looked after me back then and, to be fair, I enjoyed it.

When Danny was sacked they told me that I would never make it as a professional footballer and that hurt. I have never been back there since other than as a player for another club, but what it gave me was the strength and determination to succeed elsewhere.

I got my chance with the Millers and I loved my time there. We had a great team and I made my first-team debut in the League at just 17 against Brighton. I played at the back with Tommy Spencer and we had some class acts such as Ronnie Moore, Rod Fearn and Gerry Forrest. At one point it was like a fortress at Millmoor and we won promotion to the old Division Two. One of the big influences for me at that time was Ian Porterfield. Ian was brilliant, he knew

just how to get the best out of players and when he left to join Sheffield United I was really disappointed.

I wasn't sure what happened – I think that a few issues had occurred between him and some of the directors, but, that said, Bramall Lane was a big pull and his ambition was to be proved right. Emlyn Hughes took over and, certainly at first, did well – we just missed out on promotion to the top flight of the game and Emlyn certainly added a bit of glamour to proceedings.

I had an injury that kept me out for a fair old time – as I came back I had begun to think that the time may be right for a change. I had made 285 appearances and was still fairly young and hungry. Porterfield came in for me and I joined the Blades in 1983.

The first thing that struck me was the sheer size of the Club, it really is huge, and when you have played elsewhere it really hits home when you put pen to paper, the whole expectation level really is a different ball game in every sense of the word. Funnily enough, George McCabe, who had looked after me as a kid, was liaison officer and he remembered me well, so there were a few familiar faces.

Becoming a Blade was another important part of my development as a player, and Ian was the man to do it. I loved it from the word 'go' and he helped me take my game to another level. I would never be naïve enough to say that I was a great player, but I never gave less than 110 per cent and learned at United never to hide. The Bramall Lane crowd will forgive you a lot in the way of mistakes as long as you don't go missing – if you do they will be there to point the fact out!

The thing back then was that everyone knew you. We lived next door to fans, across the road from fans, we drank in the same pubs, shopped in the same shops – we were one. The problem these days is that there isn't the same connection – the same camaraderie. I recall when Hull City needed to win by three clear goals at Burnley to stop us going up. Myself, Keith Edwards and a few of the boys decided to meet up that night in the Royal Oak on Cemetery Road near the ground to listen to the game on Radio Sheffield and have a beer and relax. We knew if they failed we were up – many of our fans went across – we had a game of darts with a few who were in the pub. More and more filtered in as it became evident we had done it without kicking a ball – what a night that was.

Again, we had some really good players: TK, Keith, Colin – brilliant. A lot of people thought Porterfield had lost it when he started bringing in players like McNaught and Thompson, but he just wanted to try and kick us on, get to the next level with a bit of experience, it just didn't work and he left. Billy McEwan had a lot to do and he struggled. It was fading and fading fast when Dave Bassett was brought in, and 'Harry' did a great job.

I bonded with Harry straight away and he was good with me. He simplified things and it worked – things were made easy, players enjoyed playing for him and the system was very successful – the box-to-box nature of things was exciting to say the least and you had to have the accuracy to deliver good shots and crosses into the box. When we went up there were teams with better players, but we were a better team if that makes sense – a better unit that played for each other. The sum total was far better than the individual, and it counted.

I was injured for the Final decisive game at Leicester in 1990 and watched with my arm in a sling – that was the key, there was always someone who could step in – Bob Booker always thanks me in his after-dinner speeches for handing him the Captain's arm band – fair play to him! It was a great day to be skipper – I wish it had been me!! I was glad that I helped and played a part in getting the Club back, it was as simple as that. Bob wore it with pride that day.

I am so proud that I played for and Captained such an illustrious club as Sheffield United – I look back and it is with real fondness, they were great times. I still get a shout or two when shopping in Meadowhall and sometimes from fans who can't have been old enough to see me play – they must have been told by their parents!

finally, I would like to dispel a myth: if you ever get a chance to see the wonderful documentary *United* that went out on BBC Two you may recall Mrs Stancliffe dutifully pressing my grey flannels whilst my blazer hung on the door the night before a game. I would just like to point out that that was purely staged for the cameras, she never did that, and I used to end up making the spag bol as well! The glamour of a pro footballer! And I enjoyed every minute and still do. I can't wait to be there for the 125 dinners later this year.

FOOTNOTE

It is perhaps a measure of the standing 'Stan' had with fellow professionals at Bramall Lane that he not only survived the arrival and revolution of Dave Bassett but retained the armband and also led them out to battle on their return to the top flight of the English game against Liverpool on a scorching hot day in 1990. Bassett thought the same about him as everyone else did – 100 per cent reliable and 100 per cent a Club man – he would let nobody down.

I once asked him about the arrival of the *Dads Army* brigade under Ian Porterfield – I still couldn't believe that he would break up a team that many thought still had a few good years in it and replace them with some real legends who had won everything but were edging towards the end of their careers – one being Liverpool legend Phil Thompson.

They roomed together during his time at the Club and got on well. Paul had the upmost respect for the defender who had won league titles, FA, European and UEFA Cups, England Caps and a whole bag load more, as you would expect.

In their first-ever game side by side at Bramall Lane v Brighton, Thompson controlled the ball and brought it down from, what 'Stan' said, was an impossible angle, and then passed it inch perfect to him across the box. 'Stan' promptly booted it down the field to safety, turned to his teammate and asked him what the hell he was doing playing a ball like that to him in the Second Division – this wasn't Anfield – just get the bloody thing clear!!!

Stan was more than a hoofer, he was a great footballer and a cracking skipper for the Club, involved in three promotion-winning sides Bramall Lane and one at Millmoor and well respected by all in the game.

JOCK BRYSON

MILKING IT, BUT WHO IS THE ZONE MAN?

There can't be many stranger journeys to the top flight of English football than from milking cows on a dairy farm and playing part time for Kilmarnock to the Old League Division One in a relatively short space of time, but Ian Bryson made it, and in some style. Highly regarded during his time under Dave Bassett as a Blade and still involved in the game, I interviewed him during one of his regular visits back to watch Sheffield United in 2013 for the programme...

I thought my time and chance were over to play football at a higher level. I was 25 years old and had spent my entire career thus far as a part timer with Kilmarnock whilst working on the farm that belonged to my parents.

I was scouted by one of Dave Bassett's men in the shape of Colin Jackson, the old Rangers defender. He fancied me, and I got the chance to go out on the pre-season tour of Sweden that he used to like so much!

I seized the opportunity to go – it was for 10 days and I played in five or maybe six games – I must have done reasonably well because the Club offered me a deal. It was a big move for me, but I talked to Kirsty my wife and she understood as I did that this was my big chance, so the decision was an easy one.

From the off I knew it was right. There was some hold up with getting the paperwork done as the start of the season was imminent, but all was sorted, and I made my debut in the first game of the campaign against Reading. I was marked in that game by a youngster called Keith Curle – he did ok and, of course, he went on to have a great career, play for England and also pull on the red and white of the Blades as well.

To play in English football was my dream – in fact, it was the dream of many young Scottish players. It was a big step up for me, but that was made a lot easier by the Club I joined. Sheffield United called themselves the family club and with very good reason. It was so different at Bramall Lane – all the players,

backroom staff and those in the office knew each other and got on really well, the atmosphere really was something special and it gave the extra impetus to really go out and give it your all.

'Harry' was a massive influence on me, he knew just how to get the very best out of the players that he had at his disposal. His man management was second to none. In the season we went up the BBC decided to follow the team in the form of a documentary and they could not have picked a better club at a better

47

time. We were on fire on the pitch and it was a fascinating insight for all into what was to be a very special time at a great club that was coming alive again.

What a day – the Final day of that season. I will never forget the game at Filbert Street and the masses of Blades who travelled down there to cheer us over the line. We won by five goals to two – I remember a few of us panicking as every time the ball hit the back of the Leicester net our lot invaded the pitch! Being mobbed was one thing, but when it was someone in a Yogi Bear outfit or dressed as a policeman it became ever so slightly surreal

That first season back in the top flight since the mid-1970s was always going to be a tough one, but none of us thought that it would take us up to Christmas to win a game, and it came against Forest – an early Christmas present on December 22nd in front of over 20,000 people. If my memory serves me correctly, Roy Keane made his debut in that game; in fact, I think that he scored in that match. It was also the nearest that I ever came to a hat trick. Late on in the match I hit both the post and the bar!

That was irrelevant in the end as I scored two and 'Deano' got the other in our first win. I can never forget how good that game felt at Bramall Lane and, of course, it set us off on a run that saw us eventually finish a very credible 13th in the division. The Christmas win meant that 'Harry' then started the custom of having the Christmas party before the start of the season, but that was just the sort of thing he would do, it helped morale and put a smile on the faces of all involved from the off.

The Manager didn't often praise us after a game – he was more akin to battering us for what had gone wrong – that was his way and it worked. That said, he was concerned solely with the events on the pitch over the course of 90 minutes – what we got up to through the week and away from the Club didn't bother him too much, which was a good job! You would go in to see him to try and wangle a wage rise and come out with a new deal accepting less money! He really knew how to run a Club on a shoestring as far as player wages were concerned.

There were some great characters such as 'Bradders' (Carl Bradshaw), Sid Whitehouse and Mitch Ward – the 'Slaps' as they were christened – all local lads along with Jamie Hoyland and Chris Wilder who really knew what it meant to pull that shirt on – how much it mattered to the fans, and that sort of feeling and heart was invaluable to us.

The season of the Semi-Final against Wednesday saw me struggle a wee bit with injury and it was so frustrating. I played in both of the quarter-Final cup games v Blackburn and, in fact, came off at Bramall Lane with an injury. I had a double hernia operation in the December and had clearly come back too soon as I aggravated it – the match at the Lane would prove to be my last for the Club.

I sat in the stands at Wembley, as did 'Bradders', but for different reasons – he should have played that day and I couldn't. I recall how poignant it was seeing big Mel Reece lead the lads out – we had all sorts of hurdles to get over for that to happen with the FA, but it was worth it. The strength he had shown, and the courage, meant that he had more than earned it. Sadly, he passed away not too long after.

That, as I say, was my last season as a player. Harry told me that I was not going to figure in his plans as much and that he would help me get a move. Despite interest from the Millers, I joined Barnsley briefly before PNE – a Club I am still involved with to this day. Every time I see Dave Bassett I always tell him that he sold me too soon and the Club got relegated as a result!

I still love the Blades. I am proud to have played for them at such an exciting time and to have had a small part in putting them back to where they rightfully belonged – at the top of the football tree in England. As a winger, I scored 100 league goals and hit the back of the net 44 times for United; I also had the privilege of crossing the ball in for Brian Deane and Tony Agana!

A superb club with the best fans that you could ever wish to meet.

And for the record, I was the frontal zone man!

FOOTNOTE

It really was a Dave Bassett quality to find top-class footballers in places that others didn't look – think of Vinnie Jones working as a hod carrier and playing Non-League for Wealdstone not long before lifting the FA Cup for the Dons after soundly beating a top-class Liverpool side in the 1988 Final.

'Harry' was a top-class Man-Manager – he could get the very best out of a player and knew just the right buttons to press at the right time – when to put a hand round a shoulder and when to bite their ear off – it really is an art.

'Jock' appreciated the chance he was given and truly seized it with both hands. The part he played in the resurgence of the Club under the Bassett era should never be underestimated – ask any of his teammates and he really was regarded as a 'footballer's footballer', hard working, totally reliable and with a not-too-shoddy record of putting the ball in the back of the net for an absolute pittance of a transfer fee and wages.

He really did sum up the era of the game in which he played for the Blades and is one of many real gems that the then manager unearthed whilst working on a shoestring budget and also working miracles.

Still very much a part of the coaching staff at his Final league club, Preston North End, we welcome him back as a guest at Bramall Lane when his busy fixture list allows, and he is still in contact with all who know him at the Club on a regular basis.

And now you know exactly who the zone man was!

PHIL JAGIELKA

ROLLS ROYCE OR JUST 'JAGS'?

It is a measure of his affection for Sheffield United that, on the day of Sheffield United's 125 Dinner, he Captained Everton v Liverpool in the Merseyside Derby then dashed across the Pennines, back to his spiritual home, and ended up being voted runner-up in the all-time greatest player vote, behind Tony Currie – some accolade and a measure of the esteem in which the Blades Academy graduate is held by a particular generation of fans. I sat with him that evening and asked him about his thoughts and memories of his time at Bramall Lane.

I came to United in 1998 as a trainee. I had been released by Everton and had a spell at Stoke, where my brother Steve was, but it was the Blades who got my signature. I am a Manchester lad, so Sheffield was ideal – far enough away to be independent yet near enough if I needed the family. I knew it was the right place straight away – outside the Club shop on the wall I think it still says 'Sheffield United is in my blood, always has been, always will be', or at least something like that, and it has genuinely always been the case.

I liked the city from the start, and we had some great characters around Bramall Lane, both in the playing staff and backroom people. I always looked forward to every day at the ground and up at Abbeydale where we trained back then. It was Russ Slade and Kevin Philliskirk who looked after me at first, and then Ron Reid – all were great people and helped me so much as a young player.

It was the right club at the right time for many of us, and I got a chance to establish myself in the first team towards the end of the 20001/02 season, earning England Youth and eventually England Under-21 Caps along the way. Neil Warnock was the one who gave me my chance to really crack on and I took it with both hands. I recall a League Cup game against Lincoln fairly early on that we won 6-1, but it was an game away at Grimsby Town that gave me a League bow.

The youth really did get a chance – firstly because it was a financial thing – we had some good talent and it saved a fortune – and also we were ready.

Myself, 'Monty' and 'Tongy' were all fairly close in terms of age and we were all mates. We shared a house at Chapeltown, not far from the Acorn Pub, and it was an absolute nightmare, well, not the house as such, but 'Monty'. He got the nickname 'Sergeant Major' as he was so obsessed with tidiness and cleanliness – I swear that if you got up from the settee to make a drink he would puff the pillows up, place it back neat and tut under his breath. The place was immaculate – no pots in the sink, beds made, washing and ironing done – he was like Mrs Doubtfire.

The first week I moved in my own place I remember getting battered as it looked as though I had slept in my shirt – the reality was that 'Monty' had always done the ironing and I hadn't a clue – for a while it was like getting divorced!

As a player, I always felt I was a midfielder, even though Neil Warnock always maintained I was a natural defender. Most people the the Club agreed with him, but never me – just shows you what I knew as I play for England in that position now!

I was a part of the 'triple assault' season – so near yet so far, and I learned so much from Stuart McCall – a great role model and pro who had time for us all, as well as Robert Page who was a marvellous Skipper. The promotion season saw me ever present in the team and I also played every game in the Premier League for the Blades. I watched the Leeds game unfurl with the rest of the lads at Shirecliffe the day our return to the top flight was sealed, and I will never forget how we celebrated, but that was us – we did everything together and it was a great team spirit.

The open-top bus parade around the city was so sweet – we had done it in 2003 and it felt strange as we had nothing to celebrate. This time it was different and we deserved it. The celebrations on the pitch after the Final game v Crystal Palace were something I will personally never forget – Derek Dooley singing 'New York New York' with the fans joining in – I still treasure it.

'Morgs' was quoted as saying he made me the player I am today, and I can't argue with that. I watched what he did and tried not to do it myself – really simple! Joking aside, he was marvellous and a great Captain – a leader and, when the bullets were flying, he was one of the ones that you would want at your side, but we did have a great team. Paddy was as good as you could get as a keeper and there was class in all areas.

I always fancied myself in the net and would go back after dinner for training with Andy Leaning, Paddy and 'Pesch' when he was there – that meant that we never had a spare keeper on the bench back then – I think I went between the sticks on four occasions, one of those v Arsenal for the last 30 minutes when Paddy got injured, and I kept a clean sheet!

I am also proud that I managed 137 consecutive appearances in red and white. I was told that there was only a player called Jack Smith and another called Alan Woodward who have topped that. I was lucky with injuries and tended to heal quite quickly as well. It was ironic that my hand ball against Wigan resulted in the David Unsworth penalty that sent us down, and it haunts me to this day, along with all that has happened to the Club since then.

I was Young Player of the Year in 2003 and player of the season in 2005, 2006 and 2007, so to play an unwitting part in what was relegation was awful. I had turned down other transfers in the past, but I knew that as I wanted to play for my country the Premier League was the place I had to be. I had a clause in my contract that set the fee at an agreed amount and it was Everton that was my destination.

Had we stayed up then I would have remained at Bramall Lane – no doubt on that score – but I could not have picked a better place to go than Goodison Park. The two clubs are very similar, the staff are close behind the scenes and there is a family feel. I have become Captain there and I wear it with the same pride as I wore it on occasions at United.

I still keep in contact with the people with whom I became close at United and it was a pleasure to be invited to the 125 Dinner and an even bigger honour to be runner-up to TC as the greatest player. It shows the age range voting, but it was still an honour that I did not expect at all. I never forget my roots and I would dearly love to finish my playing career back where it began and in the number six of Sheffield United. It travels with me and I always think of Bramall Lane.

It has been a busy summer – the World Cup was an experience, and then, after not too big a break, it was back to the Premier League. You can guarantee that when fixtures allow I will be back at the Lane cheering on the lads.

Once a Blade always a Blade!

FOOTNOTE

At the time of writing, Phil Jagielka is still plying his trade in the blue of Everton as their Captain in the Premier League. Success can change some people, often without them knowing, but all who know him will testify that for 'Jags' this isn't the case. He has told me often that the reason he settled so well at Goodison Park was the fact that, to him, it was a home from home – like United, a family club where the staff behind the scenes know the players and their families and there is a good atmosphere – a bond between the two, and it makes a Club stronger, it really does.

'Jags' has always been a true professional – even as a youngster he knew how to conduct himself and always did so impeccably. When you are looking for a player on a Saturday night at the end of the season to go out to the back end of beyond to present junior football players (who invariably will be Wednesday or Manchester United fans) the show of willing hands can be low indeed – as a player officer the ones you could always rely on would be Phil, 'Monty' or 'Tongy' – I suspect this is because, at one time, they all shared a house at Chapletown! When he moved out into his own place I remember the day he turned up before the game and his shirt wasn't ironed properly – he admitted it was because Nick Montgomery had always done them for him in the past and he had no idea what to do!

Over a decade after leaving he is still a lad who if he doesn't answer the phone to you will call back within the hour. Despite Premier League and England honours, he has never forgotten his roots or Bramall Lane family, and that should make the Blades very proud.

BOB WIDDOWSON

ALWAYS THERE

PLEASE CHECK
SENSE - LINE 5

The days have long gone when a footballer is generally content to stay in the shadows at a Club playing reserve-team football – there was a time when the money didn't really change much if you went elsewhere and also a time when just being happy to be playing the game and enjoying it were really enough. Former keeper Bob Widdowson is the embodiment of that sort of player, and he is still working in the game today. I worked with Bob when he coached at our Shirecliffe academy and was always impressed by his professionalism and commitment to his trade. I was also surprised that he was content to stick it out here as a player, always living under the never-injured shadow of one of our greatest ever players, Alan Hodgkinson. Bob tells his story…

I was born in Leicestershire but spent most of my formative years not that far from Sheffield in Retford. I was spotted as a youngster playing by the Sheffield United scout Archie Clarke – what a job he did for United bringing in the youth that built the team of the 1960s at Bramall Lane, and what a tragedy it was when he died suddenly, he really had an eye for a player.

Initially I played football for Retford Grammar and Bassetlaw Boys – the strange thing is that I cannot recall any other who was with me at that time who made it at any other club. I would have been scouted some time in 1958, and I joined the Club in 1959 on a permanent basis. I was not, however, one of the players who came in on a Wednesday night to train, I went straight into the youth side and also played for the 'A' team.

To be quite honest, I would have been happy in the sixth form carrying on my studies, but the school didn't want to have me away and playing for Sheffield United on a Saturday as it meant that they had no goalkeeper for the school team! The choice was, in a sense, made for me. It would be professional football.

I came to a Club that already had two very good goalkeepers on its books, with Des Thompson and, of course, Alan Hodgkinson – there were also legends

like Joe Shaw, Gerry Summers, Graham Shaw, Len Allchurch and Doc Pace. The thing was that all of these players made a young lad feel so welcome, and that was the mark of the Club. Alan and Des were both a massive influence and help to me, they really took me under their wing. Don't forget 'Hodgy' was the England keeper of the time along with Ron Springett – sad to think that we lost the two of them last year so close together. How could you not learn from Alan Hodgkinson?

In my first season I played youth games and a fair few reserve ones as well – the team was the one that pushed for promotion and also got to the FA Cup Semis v Leeds. 'Hodgy' was also seldom if ever injured and probably would have kept quiet about it if he was, so I had to be patient and just get on with things. It has been said before, John Harris used to organise some unbelievable pre-season tours, and I was fortunate enough to travel on a couple of these over the years. We went out to Germany, Switzerland and Holland at the end of the 1959/60 campaign and, as Alan was away with the England squad, I played in all five games.

The first was at Basle, and I recall that it was one hell of a ground, a World Cup standard stadium that had been used for a game v Germany fairly recently. I did OK and we drew 1-1 through a Ronnie Simpson goal. By the last game I was shattered – the demands of five games in 15 days took their toll – bear in mind I wasn't even 20 at that point, but it was one hell of a learning curve.

As I have said, players didn't just move at that point – if you were happy that was a big part of things. I was playing the game I loved at a great club. In the reserve games we got crowds that many clubs around here would kill for today for a league match, don't forget that!

I got my League debut on Tuesday 3rd April away at Blackpool in a First Division game at Bloomfield Road. I must have done OK as we beat a useful tangerines side by four goals to two. Ken Mallender also made his debut in that game. These days, if a keeper took his chance and the team won you would probably be a bit miffed if you didn't keep your place – once again, you have to remember who our number-one choice was, and he was back for the next game. It was no issue waiting in the wings behind 'Hodgy' – I know that I have mentioned it already, but he was brilliant for me, as was Gerry Summers, they were dead straight people who had your best interests and that of the Club very much at heart.

I was also a cricketer, I played for many years for Retford Cricket Club and loved the game then as I do today. All know the cricket connection with the Blades and we had some good players here who would turn out during the summer, and Alan was decent, so there were other connections. I played at Retford with the great Derek Randall. He got in their side aged 15 and went on to have a decent career, didn't he?

The banter at United was also brilliant. You had to learn to take the wind-ups before dishing them out, it was all part of learning, all a part of growing up. I was at United until June 1968 and played a total of 12 first-team games and I loved my time there. It was Joe Shaw who took me to York City when he became Manager there. He liked me and rated me enough to take me with him, and I decided that it would possibly be the best move at my age. I made 30 appearances but injured my elbow and missed the second half of the season.

I also spent a little time out on loan with Portsmouth – I came across another former Blade down there with David Munks, and came across Mike Trebilcock, the Cornishman who had helped slay the other side in Sheffield in the 1966 FA Cup Final a few years before.

When I had done with League Football, I had a spell playing in Non-League and I also worked as a rep for many years for Nestle – again, I enjoyed the life. I am now in my 25th year as a goalkeeping coach and have worked at Barnsley, where I coached Dave Watson, who is now in the England fold, and then I spent some great years back at Sheffield United at the academy – I played a part with Jamie Annerson, George Long and George Willis and it's great to see George Long doing so well today, he is a great lad, professional and very focused, and I am not surprised that he is having success. I left under Kevin Blackwell and spent time at Scunthorpe and Doncaster after that.

I am now coaching the ladies at Notts County and will be 75 later this year, so I don't think I am doing too bad!

I will always love the Blades, I had a great time there and it is a huge part of my life.

FOOTNOTE

Bob made a name for himself as one of the pioneering, dedicated goalkeeping coaches, following in the footsteps once more of his friend and mentor Alan Hodgkinson, the man who really invented the role himself. He was arguably the first full-time professional who worked across the Leagues and Internationally.

He had a very successful stint at Barnsley and worked with one of the very best there of the last 30 years, Dave Watson, before re-joining Sheffield United in 2000. At the time of the interview he was enjoying coaching the Ladies at Notts

County and had worked with some of the very best, including International Karen Bardsley.

The Magpies wound up their ladies project in 2017, but there is no sign of him hanging up his gloves, that would just not be Bob at all. Handing over a lifetime of experience in the craft, I am sure that he will be around and playing his part for a long time to come. I found out that, when he spent time at Portsmouth at the end of the 1960s, he shared a flat with a certain former Everton player by the name of Mike Trebilcock.

If you are a Blade, or one of the others, the Cornishman played a hefty part in Sheffield football folkelore when he scored two to level the 1966 FA Cup Final score before Derek Temple netted the winner – Wednesday became the first-ever team to surrender a two-goal advantage in such a game after half time! Clearly, this appealed to the side of me that likes to wind others up, especially blue and white friends as a Blade!

Bob was able to secure his autograph on a replica '66 Everton Final shirt and this was framed by me and put on the wall in our local, where it stayed for many years!

ALAN BIRCHENALL MBE

THE BLOND BOMBSHELL

Ask any fan of a certain age who their favourite strikers for the Blades are, and two names will always come up: Jones and Birchenall, both controversially sold within weeks of each other for what was approaching record fees. I caught up with 'Sherman' to talk about his life at the Lane and find out what one of football's great characters is up to in the game today…

Although I was born in the East End of London I moved to Nottingham aged four and watched Notts County from the terraces with my Dad. It was strange that as a kid I played for Notts Boys with a certain Mick Jones, who would play a big part in my life later on.

I was playing for a youth club in Nottingham and looking like I would get a chance to join the County groundstaff when I literally got a tap on the shoulder from the great architect of the Sheffield United youth talent conveyor belt of the time in the shape of Archie Clarke. He said he liked what he saw and offered me a trial of three months with the Blades. I had a job at the time as an apprentice fitter in a bus garage, but it was a no brainer and I took the offer up.

I loved it at Bramall Lane from the word go. There were some great young players there and some fantastic senior pros – Sheffield United were a big Club and I was delighted with the chance and determined to seize it with both hands.

I lodged with Len Badger and his Mum Hilda; in fact, she was like a second mother to me and Len became one of my closest friends – he still is. What a great environment to be in when coming as a young lad from a different city.

I was playing in the northern intermediate side, initially in midfield, with Mick playing at centre forward. It wasn't long before 'Jonah' got his chance in the first team. John Harris had me in the office and said that I wasn't impressing in that position and he was going to give me a chance to prove myself up front or that would be that.

I played away at Hull and we won 9-2 – I got seven of the goals and we ran riot on them. I will never forget as we came off the pitch at the end of the game, their centre half shook my hand and said, 'thanks mate, you have finished my career!' He was probably right, it would prove to be the most fruitful spell in my playing years in terms of goal scoring. My journey to the first team was a strange one, I went more or less from the youth into the first-team frame.

John Harris was very brave at that time, he was a brilliant manager who realised that, in essence, a team of legends was coming to the end of its day, and he had to act quickly. Youth moved in: Bernard Shaw was challenging his elder brother and

England International brother Graham, Badger took the place of Cec Coldwell and the transition began. I was told that I would be traveling with the first team for an evening game at Stoke, a great experience for a young 'un. It was a Wednesday night game and I expected to go along, help with the kit, make drinks and so on, and I was happy to be involved. The pre-match meal was at the Grand Hotel in town – I had never seen a steak before, let alone eaten one, so I had mine and then helped myself to Joe Shaw's before eating Cec Coldwell's toast!

As if that wasn't enough, I went for a walk and there was a sweet shop nearby – I bought loads of chocolates, a few Mars Bars etc for the trip. I remember being sat at the back with Len scoffing them, Badger kept telling me to slow down, but I wasn't playing, so I was determined to enjoy the day out.

I remember getting to the Victoria Ground and reading a programme. Stan Matthews's name was in it even though he didn't play that night. John Short ,the Assistant Manager shouted me over – I didn't know that the great Doc Pace, who lived in Birmingham, had been taken ill and couldn't make the game – the lads knew but had kept it quiet from me. 'Get changed lad, you are playing.' I went cold, I thought he was winding me up. I walked in the dressing room and they all gave me a round of applause. There hung up was the famous red and white number 10 and it was mine. We won 1-0 and Mick Jones scored. In the days before mobile phones I couldn't even let my Mum and Dad know, but that is how it goes. On the Saturday we played at Hillsborough. We ran out 2-0 winners and I got both goals – I was on my way! It also signalled the end of the legendary 'Doc's' career – he never played for the Club again and soon after joined Notts County – my boyhood club.

I remember me and Len going in to town and buying a Triumph Spitfire each from a showroom – we had both saved up £500 apiece and these cars were the business – one red and one white – perfect! We tossed up for who would have which colour; I got red. We took them home to Intake and parked them under the streetlight – both dreaming of driving in the morning down the Moor to the Lane with the roofs down, regardless of the weather – we really felt like we had arrived! When we went out the following morning someone had run a key down the side of both of them – he must have been at Hillsborough the week before then!

I was regarded as the social secretary of the team even at a young and tender age. We would go out on these incredible pre-season tours that John Harris organized – 1965 we went out to Australia and New Zealand for six weeks, playing 12 exhibition games against Blackpool – it was my job to ring the local hospital up, introduce myself to the nurses and invite them to the match (and, of course, the after-game party).

The lads used to hang out in a Sheffield nightclub called the Penny Farthing – the Blades players would be the ones having a good time and a few beers (post-match of course); the Wednesday ones would be the miserable buggers sat nursing a coke! My party piece was to get up on stage and sing with Joe Cocker. Rufus Thomas's 'Walking the Dog' was a real favorite and crowd pleaser. I think I was better than Joe, but that's a different story. The lads would whistle like they were summoning a sheep dog as we sung, and as a reward I would shower them with beer. Happy days!

Not many people realise that Don Revie wanted to buy me and 'Jonah' for a combined £200,000. John Harris refused and, of course, Mick went to Leeds – the rest is history. Shortly after Dave Sexton signed me for Chelsea, and I was gone too. I loved Bramall Lane but it was too good to turn down – they were the glamour side of English football, but I always missed the camaraderie of my days as a Blade - that said I wish that me and TC had the syndication rights to the famous 'kiss' picture form 1975 – we could have both retired – it got photo of the year in one of the main gay mags!

FOOTNOTE

'Birch' is still very much a part of the game – he has been at Leicester City in various positions for 33 years. He is club ambassador and also MC on match days. Last year he was honored for his charity feats – he has raised over a million down the years and that figure is still rising as we speak, as well as presenting his own football radio show down there. One of the great characters of the era, it's great to know he is still around and involved with the game.

He is one of the funniest men you could ever meet – not only in football but the world in general. Some players just drift around clubs in a career and never really find a home or place where their heart truly sits – when Alan and Leicester

City came together it was a perfect fit. He still has an office at the training ground today in his role as club ambassador. He also found himself in the honors list for his tireless charity work whilst still finding time to be the master of matchday ceremonies pitch side for Leicester City at every home game. I think he had his own week-long party when the foxes defied all of the odds to win the Premier League.

He collapsed at an event in Leicester from a huge heart attack in 2016 and was truly fortunate that the sports centre he was at had a defibrillator and, more to the point, someone on hand that knew how to use it – it saved his life.

He is back at work doing the job he loves. This means that it makes it difficult for him to get to Bramall Lane, but if chance arises he always does. His friendship with Len Badger goes right back to the days when he lodged with Len's Mum Hilda at Woodseats then Intake in a Club house and is still strong to this day, as is his love and regard for the Club and city that gave him his chance.

MICK JONES

ON STRIKE

The Ponds Forge celebrations gave me a huge chance to catch up with so many former greats of the Lane. Mick Jones still lives near Sheffield and keeps in contact with the Blades, attending games when possible, and he always gets a warm reception when he returns to the place that started one hell of a football career. I asked him about his memories of Sheffield United and the heady days of the early 1960s youth explosion.

Mick changed the football world and turned it on its head – he was the first £100,000 footballer in the English game – a huge responsibility to have placed around your neck back then. Joining the Revie machine was a very different world to the one he had known at Bramall Lane, but one that would see him form one of the deadliest and most successful of its time with Alan Clarke.

I was born in Rhodesia near Worksop and as a kid I was taken to watch both United and Sheffield Wednesday by my uncle – I really was one of those who went to the Lane one week and Hillsborough the next, so I had no real cut-and-dried allegiances as a youngster back then. I was brought up in the village of Shireoaks where I had a happy childhood and I played football for Worksop, Dinnington Miners Welfare and also Notts Boys – that is where I first came across Alan Birchenall and a lad who never really made it as a professional but did quite well in the game by the name of David Pleat!

I first got spotted by West Bromwich Albion and had trials there. I was working in a well-known cycle factory at the same time but, to be honest, I didn't really fancy the move over the midlands, so it was great when Archie Clarke, who was scout at Sheffield United, spotted me – he was responsible for a lot of the great players at that time. I was offered the chance to train at the Lane two evenings a week, and that fitted well with my work, so to United I went.

I played in the Northern Intermediate side for the Blades and scored goals for fun – we had some fine players and I really enjoyed myself, and there were some real characters around the place like Len Badger, so all was good. John Harris was also fantastic to me – I saw Tony Currie and 'Woody' describe him as a father figure, and, to be fair, I would say that was a very good description and that is probably why he got the best out of such a young bunch of lads at the time.

67

I progressed well and made my first-team debut after four days in the easy environment of Old Trafford in a League game against Manchester United on April 20th in a 1-1 draw. Barry Hartle scored our goal in a 1-1 draw, so that was a decent result. The next game was against Manchester City, again away, at Maine Road four days later – we won 3-1 and I got a brace – 'Doc' Pace scored the other, and I was off and running!

I was so lucky as a young player. I got a chance to learn the trade of centre forward from one of the very best ever to play football in the city, and that was Derek Pace – 'Doc' always knew where to be and was so instinctive – it didn't matter whether it went in off his nose, his elbow or his arse, he would always produce. He was also a top bloke and really had an interest in what we were doing. There was also Joe Shaw, Graham Shaw, Alan Hodgkinson, Brian Richardson, all great names and all great tutors in the traditions of football and of Sheffield United FC.

Alan Birchenall then broke into the team – he made his debut away at Stoke as Pace didn't travel due to illness. Again, a bit like me, once he got his chance he was away, scoring a brace in his second game at Hillsborough. We knew each other well from junior football so it was easy to play alongside him and we formed a pretty formidable partnership.

League success brought me to the attention of the national team and I was lucky enough to win nine under-23 Caps for England. There was a great picture of me and Len Badger on our way on the train to play against Scotland wearing 'Tam-o-Shanter' hats that appeared in the press. I have a copy along with many other treasured ones of that time – it all seemed to go so quickly, just a blur to be honest. I don't think I have changed a bit, though Len hasn't worn so well!

I also won two full England Caps at United, of which I am still very, very proud. I remember playing in Joe Shaw's testimonial and getting the peg next to Jimmy Hagan in the dressing room – I was awe struck. He asked me my name and where I played – after I told him he pointed out that, at his age, he didn't run around, but if I gave him the ball when and where he wanted it he would either create an opportunity or put it away himself – not an inch to the left or right mind, right where he asked for it. The first pass was a yard wide and he went berserk with me. I spent the rest of the game making sure I did what is was told.

Jimmy went off after about 60 minutes to a standing ovation without a hair out of place. I went off at the very end knackered! In the dressing room he told me that he liked what he had seen and, if I kept working hard, then I may just have a career in the game. I was gutted, I had played for England and made well over 100 League appearances already at that point!

I wasn't given any choice when I went to Leeds – John Harris had me in his office and told me that he didn't want to lose me, but the Club had received a £100,000 offer – record equaling – from Leeds United and that Don Revie and Manny Cussins were on their way to my house to negotiate a deal and it would be best for me to go and see him.

Me and my wife had not lived there long and I well recall pulling on to the road and seeing my lawn covered with reporters. Word had got out and Leeds were very much the team of the time. There was a huge car on the drive, a Jaguar I think, and that was the car that took me to Elland Road and a changed life. I didn't want to leave United, I loved it there, but the wages were more than trebled and that, added to the fact that United needed the money, clinched the move.

It was, in football terms, the right decision. I played in a top side that saw me win the FA Cup, two League Championship medals, an FA Cup Runner-Up and Fairs Cup-Winner's medal – it was a hell of a time there and I was fortunate to strike up another great partnership with Allan Clarke. Many remember me dislocating my elbow making the cross for 'Clarkey' to score in '72 and going up (in a fair amount of pain) to get my medal.

It was a knee injury that finished me as a player – floating bone. These days it would just be washed out and you would be back and firing on all cylinders inside two months – to me it was the end. One of my last games was at Bramall Lane and I Captained the Leeds team. I shouldn't have played but the gaffer asked me to and it meant a lot. I had a cortisone injection at the Hallam Towers Hotel where we were staying. I got a great reception – then again, I always did.

The Blades will always hold a special place for me in my heart. It was the start and I owe the Club a lot. I come back when I can and still speak to Len and co, great memories – happy days.

FOOTNOTE

When I think of Mick Jones it reminds me of possibly the first FA Cup Final I ever remember kind of sitting through – not for the game but for the fact that we'd, just that week, purchased not only our first colour television, but the first on our road. As a result of this the front room was full of senior service cigarette smoke and every person Dad knew within a five-mile radius, who had all come to see the season's showpiece game on our Ferguson Colour Star (in its own wooden cabinet cunningly disguised to look like a drinks cabinet).

I remember him being helped up the 39 steps at Wembley, arm in sling, to pick up his well-earned winner's medal. Dad couldn't stand Leeds, but he loved Mick Jones and was made up that our former starlet had added another trophy to a career that he always watched and admired. Mick never changes – despite being an integral part of arguably one of this country's finest-ever club sides, he will never dodge the fact that Sheffield United has a special place in his heart. It's also interesting to note that his grandchildren have not set their allegiances up the M1 at Elland Road, but at Bramall Lane, the place that it all really started for one of the very best strikers of his era.

RICHARD CRESSWELL

ONCE A BLADE...

The last thing you need is a journeyman striker and one that has played for both Leeds and Wednesday you may think…

During his time at United, Richard Creswell typified just what it meant to play for the Club. Hard working, brave and totally honest as a pro, he never shirked responsibility and won the crowd over, picking up the official supporters' club player of the year award along the way for his troubles. When injury caught up with him he added his knowledge and support to both Danny Wilson and also Chris Morgan as a coach before moving on to pastures new.

There were a few raised eyebrows when Kevin Blackwell brought me in from Stoke City on loan to beef up the attack at Bramall Lane, all of which were from the Blades fans! I had started out with York City and been signed for the neighbours across the city as a teenager for around one million pounds. I knew that up to 'Quinny', 'Broms' and Del Geary joining, there hadn't historically been that many to play successfully for both sides of the Steel City, but for me it really wasn't a problem at all.

My time at Hillsborough was a difficult one to say the least – I was signed by Danny Wilson and went to a Club that still had a hell of a lot of big-money foreign players who were always going to be ahead of me in the pecking order, so to me that time is a bit of a blur, and I was glad to be on my way after little more than a year to Leicester City, where I finally began to get a decent crack of the whip – that said, I have nothing but good things to say about Danny – a really top bloke.

I kind of had a connection with the Blades going way back. I played in a local kid's football team in Bridlington where I grew up – they were called Bridlington Rangers and there was a lad a bit younger than me in the side by the name of Curtis Woodhouse – he didn't do too badly for himself did he? He had a mate called Lee Morris in the side who could also play a bit as well – just think, Brid

Rangers had three future England players in their ranks, that must be a bit of a record, and both would, of course, go on to make their mark at the Lane. I also came up against the formidable frame of Christopher Paul Morgan when playing for the county side as he did for South Yorkshire boys – I still have the scars to prove it!

I made my debut for the Blades v Doncaster Rovers, and what a baptism of fire that was – not only had I played for the Old Enemy, I had, of course, also played for Leeds. In the eyes of many a Blade, I was exactly the sort of player they didn't want, and they made it very clear that was the case.

The thing with Blades is that they like someone who always gives 120 per cent, and quite right too. I never hid in my entire career – I was always prepared to give my all in the field of battle. I scored in the Donny game and in the process wrapped myself around the goalposts and seriously damaged a couple of ribs. I played on – that's what it is all about at the end of the day, isn't it? I think that this went a long, long way to breaking the ice with the terraces, and I am really glad that it did.

We just missed out at the end of that year on the play-offs in the Final game away at Southampton. We had a great team and no mistake. It was a fine dressing room, one of the best that I have ever been in, and we all knew that the Club and chairman would have a proper go at it the following season.

Have a go at it we did. We were on fire at times and it culminated in the play-off Final against Burnley – and the rest, as they say, is history – I was devastated, and that set off the chain of events that saw Blackie dismissed after two games, 'Speedo' depart after a few months for the Wales job, and then Mickey Adams have the unfortunate record of taking Sheffield United down to the Second for the first time in well over 20 years, and it hurt.

Danny Wilson was a breath of fresh air when he came in, and I can honestly say that the season that followed was the best of my career – amazing stuff coupled with the fact that it was also the best bunch of lads I had the pleasure of sharing a dressing room with in the course of my long career. I enjoyed every day.

People I met at Bramall Lane are my friends for life and I keep in close touch with a good many of them on a regular basis. 'Morgs' is a top man,

'Monty' is Monty, the kind of player that every team needs and you don't miss him until he isn't there any more – I am sure that you know what I mean by that – I still speak to plenty of the backroom and club staff as well.

That season we were the leading goal scorers in Europe, and the will to play and win was so strong. I played a fair few games with a badly dislocated shoulder that could and often did pop out on a regular basis. The team that season named itself game in, game out and I know that a good many fans told me it was the best football they had seen played at Bramall Lane in many years, and it always makes me feel really good when I hear that.

When I say good memories that's correct to a point – the end of the season and Wembley was terrible, the knock-on effect of other events that had come into play the day before an important away game at MK Dons that shook the Club and dressing rooms to the very core. No game should have to end with a penalty shootout after a season like that; 'Simmo' will always get stick for it, but it's undeserved – it was just the finger of fate pointing at the Blades once more and finding a scapegoat.

I am a Blade through and through, make no mistake about that. Of all the Clubs that I played for, Sheffield United is the one that really got under my skin, the one that got to my heart. I loved my time in those famous stripes. The Blades are completely different, and it was like having one huge extended family – the years that I spent there were special to me, the very best, and it became a part of me. It's rare that happens in football, but ask 'Morgs', 'Monty' and many others how they feel, and I suspect that you will get a very similar answer. What's the saying? Once a Blade always a Blade – I've heard that before and it really sums it up.

It was good to get out on loan initially, and even better that it was with York, my first club. When I came back it was also an honour to help 'Morgs' out for that brief spell as a member of the coaching staff when he stepped into the breech – it hurt when I left – I was gutted, but life has to go on.

At the moment I am enjoying the rest. I have a very young family, one that didn't always see a lot of me, so I am making up for that for a while and I am glad to do just that. I have a couple of offers in the game that I am considering as we speak – I don't really see myself uprooting the family at any time soon, so it would have to be local.

I would dearly love to get a chance one day to come back behind the scenes and play a part at Sheffield United at some point.

Great City, great fans – my favorite Club. Proud to be a Blade and always will be.

FOOTNOTE

'Cress' went back to York and did some coaching whilst also helping out at academy level. He is still involved in the game, periodically working on projects in the USA. His eldest son is also now working hard and doing very well coming through the ranks at Leeds United. No easy task following the footsteps of a successful father in the game.

He is invited back to the Club each season to watch the game from the luxury of the TC10 suite as a guest, an invitation he always readily accepts, and is welcomed by former colleagues and fans with open arms. There aren't many strikers like him left now. The game is changing, as is the way in which players are coached. Sometimes you need a warrior and that is exactly what he was in a red and white shirt.

The Lane faithful take some time to warm to anyone who has worn the colors of the other side of the City – you have to earn their trust and respect, but it would be fair to say that he did just that in the time he was with the Club.

Once a Blade always a Blade is a very sweeping statement, but one that comes from the same heart that was worn on his sleeve during the time he was a player, and a message he still gives out to all in football to this very day.

ALAN WOODWARD

WINGING IT

One of the best parts of the incredible 125th celebrations was getting Alan Woodward over from America to be a part of the festivities. Living there in Tulsa since the late 1970s, his visits had become less frequent, and it was vitally important that one of our greatest ever players was there, side by side with many of his former colleagues for the occasion. His visit lasted three weeks and I sat down with him in the Copthorne Hotel at his spiritual home of Bramall Lane to talk about his career...

I was born in Chapeltown but I grew up in Silkstone Common; in fact, my brother Nigel is still fairly local and I have other family in the area still. I played for Barnsley Boys as a kid and I really enjoyed it, we had some great players including Jimmy Greenhoff at that time and I did well for them. So much so that I had a fair few clubs in the area who were after my signature as a youngster.

We went to meet Sheffield Wednesday, me, Mum and Dad – back then the set up was brilliant and they had been there or thereabouts in terms of the League. Eric Taylor was a lovely man and a real driving force for them over a long time, but he was back upstairs and Vic Buckingham was manager. I remember being in the office talking to him, and it may seem strange, but the thing that really sticks out in my mind is that he had most of his dinner down the front of his tie, it looked awful and it really put me off signing for them!

Leeds were keen, but United sent John Harris's car to pick us up and take us to the Lane – United just felt right. John was a great man and the Club had a reputation for promoting the youth, it felt right to me and I signed. Simple as that really.

It had been Archie Clarke who had spotted me; in fact, Archie signed a fair few of us who went on to make first-team appearances for the Blades – he had a great eye for a player did Archie, and he was a big loss to the Club when he died.

IN OTHER WORDS

I made my debut in the reserves when I was 16 and that was away at Maine Road in April 1963, but my first-team bow was in a County Cup game, and I did pretty well. I got my chance away at Anfield, along with Barry Wagstaffe, on October 7th 1964 – we lost 3-1 and Alan Birchenall scored, but I was off and running taking the number seven from John Docherty, and I never really looked back from that moment on. I played in some fine United sides, but I look back and realise that I started out in the same team as Alan Hodgkinson, Joe Shaw, Graham Shaw, Keith Kettleborough and Brian Richardson to name a few. Cec Coldwell was also a big influence on the young 'uns like me as well – I was very lucky.

We always seemed to sell our best players – Mick Jones went to Leeds, 'Birch' went to Chelsea and both for record-equaling fees, and the tragedy was that we were never that far away from a real team that was challenging for something. I had a few times where I could have gone, but I wasn't bothered. I loved being a Blade and had great friends like Len Badger with me, so it was an easy choice to stay. John Harris also turned down a couple of bids from Don Revie for me; he said there was no way he was letting me go, so maybe I was the one that bucked that trend.

Tony Currie came in 1968 and we quickly developed one of those rare relationships where it just clicked. He has said that I am the best player he ever played with, and I have agreed with him on that score many times! Seriously, though, he was different class, but you don't need me telling you that. He knew where I would be and vice versa. It just worked and worked well – it was a pleasure to play in that team and we entertained. It was and is a great bunch of lads – we all stay in touch and that was one of the reasons that I would have been here without question for the 125th anniversary dinner. Martin Green, one of the Club vice presidents, along with a few of the backroom staff, also played a very big part, so I thank them as well for that.

There is always the story that I would have a smoke at half-time in the dressing rooms – I would like to say that is rubbish – I would have two or sometimes even three if I could – to be fair the toilet had a cough! Len blames me for the fact that he has chest problems and a dicky ticker – the chest is from my smoking habit down the years and travelling together, the heart from the fact that he reckons for 14 years he would go on the overlap screaming for the ball and I gave it to him a total of three times! I have told him that was because he was rubbish and that he should have got back in position by the way! When we meet up we always have a sweep to see who will be the next one to leave us, and I have Badger down at 2-1 on! It's a tradition and I thought it was going to pay out when he collapsed after the Leyton Orient game – boy did I panic along with everyone else – I have warned him not to do that again!

I am proud that I am the post-war record goal scorer. I always felt that I could get one and could be selfish – get it in the back of the net – that is what it is all about. I wasn't bad from the corner flag either as it went! I also think I am the third-highest appearance maker for the Club, and that is also a big honour. I am in some illustrious company there as well and the way the game is these days it will probably stand for a long time.

When my time at the Lane was over, Harry Haslam was wonderful to me. I had some personal problems and needed to get away and make a fresh start. Harry was brilliant and I got a move to the States to Tulsa Renegades and played in the NFL, seeing players like Eddie Colquhoun out there. Roger Davies from Derby was in my team and I still help out with reunions. After that I had a spell as a Gridiron kicker – I just came on to do that – and I loved it. Those boys are big units you know – it isn't just padding!

I did 30 years working in the stores for American Airlines and, bizarrely, I have now lived in the States longer than I lived over here, and I still see Keith Eddy and David Bradford – they live near me. I love coming home when possible. The last time was a few years ago when my Mum passed away. The problem is that I find it hard to leave and go back. I have really enjoyed the last three weeks seeing friends, family and, of course, United.

I was quite ill a couple of years ago and, for a time, it was touch and go, but I feel good now. Hopefully you haven't seen the last of me at Bramall Lane yet! Thanks to all the fans who made it wonderful to be home, but I am gutted to be leaving after the awards empty handed after travelling so far – I mean, who is this Tony Currie feller anyway?

FOOTNOTE

Alan was always great company when he came home, despite protesting his love for the States you could see that he was back where he belonged on a visit – South Yorkshire and Bramall Lane. His son Shaun is one of my oldest friends. Through him and my years at the Club, Alan became a good friend and I was lucky to share more than a few beers in his company over the years. After the 125 event, Alan returned back to the States – I told him he was better here. Many of his family are still in the area and the love our fans had for him was incredible – a journey from the hotel on the day of a game took an hour to cover a few yards in distance – autographs, selfies, a handshake and thanks for the memories. Like many of his fellow players of that era, 'Woody' was bemused that people were still interested.

That visit was made more poignant by the news late one May evening the following year that he had passed away at home in his sleep. The player that took my memories from the black and white of childhood with Dad, to the colour and anticipation of the friendly against River Plate that I attended with my mates had joined the Higher League and done so far too soon. Alan was a gentleman and, to me and many others, one of the greatest players ever to pull on those famous red and white stripes. I am just glad that he came home one last time and hope that he died knowing just how much he meant to every Blade lucky enough to have seen him play. The last paragraph of his interview now seems so sad, written in an afternoon when we never stopped laughing.

ROBERT PAGE

FRONT-PAGE NEWS

As Former Player-Officer and One-Time First-Team Player Officer, I am fortunate to still be in touch with many players of recent times – one of the most popular of the last 20 years or so was Robert Page. A towering Captain at a time of change under Neil Warnock, Rob still lives in Sheffield today, over a decade after leading the Club to its fabled 'Triple Assault Season' when United reached the Semi-Finals of the FA Cup, League Cup and also the Play-off Final v Wolves. After his playing career ended he carved out a career as manager with Port Vale and then Northampton Town. As we speak he is a key member of the Wales FA set-up and in charge of the Under-23s. Rob takes up the story back in 2014…

I started out with Watford as a youngster, journeying up to join as an apprentice when I left school. It was a big move from the Valleys to Hertfordshire back then, but it had a real family feel to life at Vicarage Road and I loved it there. I made my debut under the eye of Kenny Jackett, who was brilliant to work under and was also a great bloke.

I was also privileged to be managed by Graham Taylor in his second spell with the Hornets. Taylor was a Club legend. He, under Elton John, had taken the Club from the Fourth to the old First back in the day before spells at Villa, the England job and Wolves. Watford was his spiritual home and he took the Club back to the Premier League via the Play-off Final v Birmingham City – that was a proud day. We were there one season, it was one of those things and I well recall scoring against Sheffield Wednesday. I was voted player of the season and again that was special.

Vialli came in and things changed. One of his first jobs was to transfer list me, and he put a fee of a million on my head. I didn't really get a chance. Neil Warnock came in for me at Sheffield United and I clicked with him straight away. I knew the potential at Bramall Lane and Neil was similar in many ways to Graham Taylor – a great man-manager who knew just how to get the best

out of his players. United also had a feel about it. It was a great stadium to play at and the fans were known for their passion. It was perfect, and I couldn't have picked better.

I joined initially on loan in August 2001 whilst the paperwork and deal between the two clubs was sorted. It meant that I could also play, which is what it was all about, and I made my debut at the City Ground v Forest on 11th August in a 1-1 draw. I quickly gelled with Shaun Murphy – we had a great bunch of lads and the gaffer was really beginning to put something very good together. It was a great place to be and we settled very well in Totley – the area of Sheffield I still live in today.

I was voted player of the year and I was so pleased to have that accolade given, of course. I also got the skipper's armband at the Club as well, but better things were to come in 2002/03. I don't think that anyone around the Club could have foreseen the 'Triple Assault Campaign' and the games that were played will always live very much in my memory. We had some great young talent coming through such as 'Monty', Michael Tonge and, of course, Phil Jagielka, but Stuart McCall's arrival was also a masterstroke. His experience and calming influence on the pitch and in the dressing room made a huge difference to what we were aiming for.

We were robbed by some strange refereeing decisions at Anfield in the League Cup Semi-Final second leg. In the FA Cup Semi against Arsenal at Old Trafford we were magnificent. I will never forget the noise from the Stretford End as we walked down the famous tunnel onto the pitch. What a Club, it showed the world what Sheffield United were capable of on its biggest stage – again, 'Chief' being flattened was a turning point along with the Ref's 'assist'. You couldn't do anything about the save, any other time or place 'Pesch' would have buried that ball, he was the master poacher in those situations, but Seaman pulled off a world-class save, and the rest is history.

The Play-off semi is one of the greatest games of them all – what a night that was, and I know that it still gets talked about today, and quite rightly so. It was a good team that was physically very fit and never ever gave up. You look at the number of goals scored late on in matches back then. We went to Cardiff in the Final but didn't turn up as a team. Had Michael Brown buried that penalty

I think we may have found a way back in. When that didn't happen, it sapped anything left out of us. He had been brilliant that season, scoring for fun, so I didn't blame him. It had been a long one with many games and it proved to be a game too far on the day. I was gutted. Shaun Murphy's wife was ill, and they decided it best to go back to Australia for treatment, and he was a loss. Always steady, strong and reliable I played well with him, but Neil pulled off a masterstroke by signing 'Morgs' from Barnsley that summer – another top lad and still a good mate.

The gaffer eventually let me go, and I joined home-town club Cardiff – that could have been a masterstroke as both of our families were near, but my then-wife didn't want to leave Sheffield! As a result, I had the bizarre situation of quite quickly looking for a move back up North!

Micky Adams signed me for Coventry City and then I had spells with Huddersfield Town and Chesterfield before I joined up with Micky again at Port Vale. This year and following his departure, I had a spell as Vale caretaker-boss before being appointed on a permanent basis at Vale Park, and I am loving the role of manager.

Many will know that I was in the running for the job at the Lane before David Weir was appointed – I would have been honoured to have had the chance at the time, but it just was not to be, that's how it goes I suppose and it has worked out well for me. I am really happy

I keep in touch with many of the people I worked with at Sheffield United, in fact many of the staff are still there, and I try and get to games when life allows, once a Blade and all that. I loved the Club and my time there, and I love the city – it has been a good home to me and my family. I was inducted to the Watford Hall of Fame, a real honour, but I am still here, and that is for a reason.

When we lost Gary Speed I was present at the tribute game. I played many times for Wales with him and was a true gent. I carried the wreath out to the centre circle and stood side by side with players and staff as he was remembered. That doesn't seem like three years ago as we speak. The club showed its class as usual that day.

I look forward to seeing the Blades on Boxing Day. The club is Premier League in every sense and I hope that Nigel gets them back up there. I know

Mal Brannigan very well also, and with 'Morgs' involved alongside others you have a great backroom there Chris would die for Sheffield United. I just hope we get a win every time we meet – apart from that it will always be very much a case of UTB in the Page household.

FOOTNOTE

It is perhaps a measure of the city and Sheffield United Football Club as a whole that Rob Page still resides here and, if pushed, will tell you that, despite his career at Watford and the fact he was voted as one of their Hall of Fame players, there is only one team that still pulses through his veins, and that is the Blades.

It has been documented that he came close to getting the Manager's job prior to the appointment of David Weir; in fact, the deal was all but done before a change of heart at board level saw the Scot briefly take the seat. He was asked to consider working in tandem and went as far as meeting him for a talk about ideas and aspirations in a Manchester hotel, but it became evident that, in his words, it just would not work.

Nothing personal, just two people with a very different vision of what should be.

He followed Chris Wilder at Northampton Town, taking with him former Blades colleague Paddy Kenny as goalkeeping coach, but he and the Cobblers parted terms after a difficult spell. You get the impression that Wales and the boy from the Valleys who made his home in the city of steel really is a great fit. His job means that he gets to watch a fair few games at his beloved Bramall Lane, largely due to the fact that he was able to play a part in encouraging Blades prodigy David Brooks that his future in International Football lay in the land of the dragon and the daffodil and not that of the Three Lions.

EDDIE COLQUHOUN

PROMOTION IS STILL SOON!

Few players names will still be sung about from the terraces some 40 years since they last played for the Club in question, and maybe that is testimony to the quality of the player involved.

I am fortunate to know or have known most of the players from the John Harris side who excited and entertained fans around the end of the 1960s through to the early 1970s, and who won promotion in such style, but the Captain was one of those who held it all together, and Eddie Colquhoun was some Captain. The former Scottish International has a love for the Club that far outstrips any of his other employers in the game. He still lives in South Yorkshire and attends Bramall Lane when possible. I caught up with him for the programme around the time of United's 125th anniversary celebrations over a cup of tea at his Conisborough home to talk about his football career...

My first English club was Bury, and I joined then in 1961. Even before becoming a Sheffield United player I had a Blades connection in so much as I was signed by the great Jimmy Hagan for West Bromwich Albion in February 1967. I had played for another great name in the shape of Bob Stokoe at Bury by the way. As a youngster I played in the game v Sunderland that saw the great Brian Clough break his leg, an injury that would end his playing career but see him become one of the greatest managers of his generation. It was a terrible injury.

I think I am one of the only players to not play in an FA Cup Final and still receive a Winner's Medal. I had played in every round of the cup in my second full season at the Hawthornes and missed out on the big day with a broken leg – that is how it goes in the game. When the Baggies lifted the famous trophy, I sat in the stands and as a mark of my contribution special dispensation was given and I got a gong – a great gesture.

I lost my place in the West Brom team as a result of that injury, and when Sheffield United came in for me it was a simple choice to join the Blades, and one that I never regretted. Arthur Rowley was the manager and he had just taken over from John Harris. Arthur had brought some top players in very quickly such as Ted Hemsley. TC was already there and stalwarts like Len Badger and 'Woody' were around – a top squad and a huge Club.

I was appointed Captain within about a week of joining – in fact I took the armband from Len, and that was a great honour for me. 'Badge' is still the youngest Captain for the Club in the League and was one hell of a player, so to think that I was deemed good enough to do the job for a Club like Sheffield United really was something. In fact, I would do the job until the 1973/74 season when Ken Furphy took the Manager's role on in December. He felt that TC was his man – again, that is how it goes in the game and it is all about opinions at the end of the day, isn't it?

I remember my first game clearly – it was away at Huddersfield Town on 19th October 1968 – Leeds Road was always a hard place to be and we lost the game by one goal to nil, and I played at the side of Welsh International Dave Powell. 'Enoch', as we called him, was a fine player as well – he had joined just before me from Wrexham, another player picked up during Rowley's brief time in charge at the Club.

My home debut was a little better, however – that was against Charlton Athletic and we won that by two goals to nil at the Lane. 'Addo' got one and there was a rare Ted Hemsley goal as well – that sticks out in my mind there!

I settled in very quickly. Sheffield and the surrounding areas were superb. I liked it that much that I still live in South Yorkshire today – the people have always been great to me and that counts for so much in life.

We finished ninth in my first season and the board decided that Rowley wasn't the man for the job. He was a quiet man and very fond of the horses, and it was said that, under his management, results were inconsistent. That said, he also had an eye for a player and many of those that he brought in, me included, would play a big part in promotion a couple of seasons later.

John Harris came back from the role of General Manager to take charge of the first team again. A quiet man, but one that was held in the highest esteem by fans and players alike, so the transition was a seamless one.

As we went for promotion in 1970/71 we could all tell that we had something a bit special going on. We entertained with the style of football that we played and had some formidable players in that side. Powell picked up an injury against QPR that would effectively end his career at Bramall Lane in much the same way as my own had been curtailed at

West Brom. His replacement in the side was John Flynn – he had been the last player signed for the Club by Rowley, and we would go on to form a great partnership and a back four that picked itself along with Ted and Len – happy days.

The Final game at home to Watford sealed promotion, and it felt so sweet. I will never forget going up into the stand after the game to applaud the fans. *The Star* did a promotion special to celebrate our achievement and I seem to remember that there is a picture of me applauding everybody with a fag in my hand – fans still remember that image – a Captain of what we would now call a Premier League team having a smoke on a day of triumph! Things have changed these days. Many of the team were smokers and it wasn't frowned upon as today, it was part and parcel of things. Alan Woodward used to have them at half time to calm his nerves – and what an athlete he was – what a player. How 'Woody' never got an England Cap is one of the great mysteries to me. Different class and no mistake.

I tried to lead on the pitch by example. I always had pace and could put a challenge in – I always played football as I felt it should be played. I would consider myself as being hard but at the same time very fair, but again the game has changed so much, I would imagine that I would fall foul of the odd decision if I was playing now!

The first season back in the First started off so well, and, of course, we all went to Old Trafford at the very top of the table – it was incredible. The team coach could not get to the ground because of the thousands walking up there for the game – it was a lock out at a ground like that, which was and still is huge. People don't believe you when I say that we had to walk the last half a mile or so and carry the big wicker kit baskets between us. Can you imagine that? Tony Currie and co all lifting the stuff that we needed, doing it by hand – you wouldn't see a team doing that these days, would you?

I also picked up nine International Caps for Scotland whilst a Blade – I think I am possibly the only International Footballer to come from Prestonpans where I was born, and, do you know, I never got a Cap from the Scottish Football Association for any of the games. Apparently, at that time they had stopped! But I was fortunate to play in some great matches. I also kept injury free. I think that in my first seven years at the Club I missed only a handful of games [it was 15 FL].

Overall, I made 430 full appearances for Sheffield United before my time as a Blade was over in the late 1970s, and I played my last game in the red and white stripes against Stoke in March 1978 before joining Detroit Express and then Washington Diplomats over in the States, as many players did at that time, and it was an incredible experience for me, Maureen and the kids.

I returned home and settled on the outskirts of Doncaster where I still live today. I retired a while ago, but I find plenty to fill my time in. One of my grandsons is a part of Rotherham United and is doing very well. I watch him as much as I can and occasionally go to the New York stadium.

As many will know, I also come home to Bramall Lane as much as I can, although it did take me a long time. I always believe that you should move on in life and not dwell on the past. My football trophies and the stuff I collected are stored away; in fact, I couldn't tell you where they are, although my missus will know!

I am proud of my time at United and always will be – I love coming back, and the recent 125 celebrations were fantastic. I still can't get over the fact that fans that never saw me play sing my name, I think they are mad, but that doesn't mean to say that I don't think it's wonderful!

It's a great club and I think that the manager will take them up next year, and I will be really looking forward to being there when it happens.

FOOTNOTE

Eddie still lives quietly in his home near Doncaster and attends games during each season. Over the years of knowing him, I found out that over the course of his Scotland career, as he didn't play in all of the old Home Internationals he had never received an International Cap for his services, as it wasn't their practice to award one. I decided this needed putting to rights, and after several conversations with the Scottish FA, coupled with getting a copy of his birth certificate from his wife Maureen (under false pretenses I may add), it was arranged that a special

Cap commemorating his service to his country would be made, to be presented as a surprise at the Club's 125th Anniversary Dinner.

Stuart McCall, then manager of Motherwell, agreed to drive down in person after his game that afternoon against Rangers to do the honors on our behalf. Eddie was invited on stage along with Alan Woodward and Tony Currie, then the surprise was sprung on a bemused Eddie in front of 1,500 people.

It is one of the most fulfilling things I have ever done in Football and the Cap is treasured by one of the game's most modest men.

CHRIS WILDER

TUFTY'S TALE

My interviews for the Club programme gave me the chance to speak to many former players from a variety of different eras – the last 30 years have seen many local lads get the chance to play for the Club. Chris Wilder was one who took an unorthodox route to the Lane as a player and now has earned a formidable reputation as a gaffer himself. Little did we know, as friends going back many years, that it would be a relatively short time before the chance to manage his beloved Blades came calling. History shows that it was a match made in heaven. In his first season he led them to the League Championship with a record number of points and re-united a Club that had lost its way with its fans. His second season saw a top-half finish. He is a manager who wears his heart and pride very much on his sleeve. 'Tufty' tells his tale…

I was born in Sheffield, although we lived in London for about four years due to Dad's work. We had lived at Richmond, amongst other places, and when we came back the choice of schools were basically Ashleigh and Hurlfield for where we lived. Mum and Dad had a sports shop at Arbourthorne by now, and Dad used to play football for the Feathers on Prince of Wales Road with the careers master at Silverdale – I think he must have thought the school football team was a bit light because he got me in there. I mean, Ashleigh had Tony Daws and John Beresford amongst others.

I knew Bez really well. I used to kick around a ball with him on the playing fields and there were some good lads around schools' football in the city at that time. The year above, which was Darren Bradshaw etc, won the Gillette Schools Trophy at Bramall Lane v Coventry City, and I think that Carl's year, the one below, may have also done so. Either way, my year didn't manage anything!

I was a Blade and still am. I had ball-boyed at games and when I came to the age of 14, playing for Sheffield boys, the United scout wanted me to sign

for the Club I supported – then things went a little away from where I thought they would.

Dad knew Stewart Houston, who at that time was Captain of Sheffield United. He told Dad not to let me sign under any circumstances as things in the youth set-up were not that good. Somehow Dad got Kevin Keegan's telephone number and made contact with him – things must have gone OK because I was invited down to Southampton for trials. I liked them, and they seemed to like me. When I was 16, Lawrie McMenemy signed me on pro-forms and away I went to Hampshire.

There really were some good lads at the Saints back then. Rod and Ray Walllace, Matt Le Tissier, Francis Benali, Allan Tankard – plenty of them – I think 10 out of 12 went on to make their name in League football, some with Southampton, others with a host of different clubs. Alan Shearer was a little bit younger and on his way through the ranks. I think you could say that they had a fair youth set up back then!

There were some great players in the first team: Peter Shilton, Mark Wright, Andy Townsend – all brilliant, and despite the quality of youth it was hard to force your way into contention. A change of manager also didn't help as Chris Nichol, a former player at the Dell, took the reigns over.

In my time there I never made a first-team appearance, and I was chomping at the bit to get my chance. It is funny in football how sometimes fate plays a strange hand. Southampton signed Gerry Forrest from Rotherham – he in turn tipped off his friend Billy McEwan off about me and I was invited to Sheffield over the course of the summer for a trial.

It was mad to be honest. A Sheffield lad back in his home city and here I was taking part in pre-season training, running around Graves Park. To be fair I knew the area really well and it was a strange homecoming in many ways. I think my first game was v Sheffield Club at Abbeydale Park and I was up against a lot of my mates!

Billy had the job of trying to change the way United had been doing things. Ian Porterfield had begun to bring in older established pros and it hadn't really worked that well. Billy brought in the likes of me, Peter Beagrie – a little later Mark Todd came in along with Tony Daws and Kevin Philliskirk. Also, around were Chris Marsden, Simon Grayson, Brian Smith and David Frain. In my first year they blooded a lot of young players and it went fairly well for us. The following year was a different story and the manager had a tough time, we had a really bad run of results and he lost his job. The choice of replacement was, of course, 'Harry' Bassett.

I had some great times under 'Harry', but I didn't think I was really going to be his cup of tea. I really liked him and his management, and he did a great job at United – it was a real team unit and players like Dane Whitehouse came through with Mitch Ward a bit later alongside great buys like Brian Dean and Tony Agana. At one point I shared a house with Brian and Bob Booker – those were happy days.

I was fortunate to be a part of two promotion teams and the day at Leicester will rate as one of the greatest of my life – what a day that was. There were Blades fans in the team as well as me and to do the job on the last day at Filbert Street was an incredible memory, made even better by the demise of our neighbours – priceless!

After the game we struggled to get into the car park back at Bramall Lane and it was even harder to get back into town after for a drink. I just remember London Road being closed – it was the biggest street party ever. In the top flight the battle for a place was really tough, with players like John Pemberton and Colin Hill around, but I was still young, happy and content to fight it out.

Dave Bassett made me Captain v Southampton – he didn't tell me until it was time to take the team sheets down, and it meant a lot. Chris Nicholl had let me go, so to stand outside the ref's room with him as a skipper in the top flight meant the world, as did the result that day. We were 4-0 up in no time – Gary Arrmstrong chose the picture of me and Bob Booker for the cover of his Blade Runner book a few years ago – it was a top day and I will never forget how good it felt to prove their manager wrong.

I left to get first-team football. Rotherham was great for me, as was Notts County and Bradford City – the Bantams were really good, and I loved it there, but they had a panic sale and on the same day got rid of me, Eddie Youds and Peter Beagrie – Steve Thompson, who I had played with, brought me back to Bramall Lane. Heart ruled head – I knew I was coming back as a squad player but it was home. We had a good cup run, but I missed out because I was already tied with Bradford – that said, I am really proud to have had two opportunities to have pulled the famous shirt on.

I still keep in contact with the lads and a lot of the staff, we had something really special at Bramall Lane, a real togetherness from top to bottom, and I think that is sadly missing from football these days as players get more detached from their roots. I have managed a few clubs and am now at Northampton, a great club with a top set up. That said, if ever we are without a fixture and United are at home, there is only one place that I will be…

FOOTNOTE

In May 2016 Chris Wilder became the Manager of Sheffield United FC after winning the League with his Northampton Town side. It was an inspired choice for both parties as those who pull on the shirt now understood exactly what it means.

A new generation was given its own Darlington, its own Leicester, its own special memories as Chris and the boys confirmed promotion on a red-hot day at his former club Northampton, followed by the Championship trophy a short time after. Thousands lined the streets from the Lane to the Town Hall to cheer the open-top bus on its way to the Town Hall civic reception – the fans got their pride and self-belief back, as did the Club. Sometimes what you wish for does come true, and it's some journey from ball boy to gaffer.

CHRIS LUCKETTI

ONE DAY SON, YOU WILL PLAY FOR US!

Chris Lucketti was one of those players who you always felt you would one day see in a United shirt. Tough, uncompromising and a great leader on the pitch for all of his Clubs, the call to join the Blades came late, but it was one that he seized with both hands. I tracked 'Lucky' down to Fleetwood, where he was assistant manager to long-time friend Graham Alexander for the Cod Army.

I had a relationship with Neil Warnock that went back to our days at Bury, and I had always kept in touch with him. Neil has a way with his lads both current and ex, and I always enjoyed playing with him. There had been more than one occasion when he had told me how much he would like to bring me in, but there was always an issue with budget or potential wages, so it never really got around to happening. That said, it was nice to know that he rated me.

I was Captain at PNE – again, it was a top club, and at that time we had been really going for it and had a decent squad. I was proud that I wore the skipper's armband at Wembley in the Play-off Final, although sadly it was not our day.

The Blades were really going all out for promotion when we played them at Deepdale on a Friday night. The game was live on Sky and I was keeping the bench warm that night, I had been banned for a couple of games and the gaffer had decided to stick with the team and that was fine. If I could help in any way then no worries.

Neil spoke to me after the match to see what was going on and if I was happy there. Basically, he was looking to bolster the squad for the Final run in and wanted me to come over to Bramall Lane to add cover for the defence as well as keeping them on their toes – no mean feat when 'Morgs' and 'Jags' were on fire at that time.

Did I fancy it? Of course I did! I saw it as being possibly my last chance to play for a Club the size of Sheffield United, and that's nothing against Preston, Huddersfield or any of my former employers . I had a great relationship with the

fans at them all. Neil got wheels in motion and I came to be a Blade on loan to
the end of the season, with the option for the Club to offer me a year extension.
This was basically the same deal as at Deepdale, so I joined.

It was a great dressing room, so strong and full of character. I was also in a position where I knew many of the lads and I had played against them on plenty of occasions, so the transition was easy.

Neil has put together a hell of a squad, built to do exactly what it did. There was some great young talent in there and he had also added players with a wealth of experience in the shape of me, David Unsworth, Adi Akinbiyi, Neil Shipperley and Craig Short, to name a few. I had been at Bury with Paddy Kenny when he was a youngster. He had a lot of rough edges back then, but you could see that he had the makings of a top-class keeper, and he proved that at Bramall Lane.

I had always enjoyed playing there with other clubs – a proper ground with a great atmosphere – exciting times.

My chance to start came against Leeds United on a Tuesday night. It was, of course, a sellout. Now, I have played in some big games down the years, but I have never played in anything quite like that. I still talk about it today. The Blades fans that night were incredible – promotion nearly in the bag and it was a real party. It was special and amazing to be a part of it all – what a night!

The next season was, of course, the Premier League, and I knew that I was there as a cover player, but that was fine. I had never been a part of a top-flight squad, so if this was my last shout I was going to really enjoy the experience. The balance and blend of the promotion side was just right – probably the best I have seen, and we took that level of expectation into the new season.

My chance eventually came when Sky cameras managed to help get 'Morgs' a ban for his altercation with Van Persie. The ref had seen nothing, but it was trial by television. The gaffer had me in and told me that I was playing against Pompey – again, and as you would expect, it was a full house and I was skipper, given the chance to help shackle players like Kanu and Cole – it was a 1-1 draw, and I played quite well!

I am, apparently, the oldest player to be a first-time Captain of the Blades, and I am quite happy with that as a stat. I also think that I am the oldest player to make his Premier League debut as well, and I think that there is a lesson in that for every young and aspiring footballer – never give up no matter what, there is never a limit to what you can achieve – I have been both promoted and relegated out of every League, so I am living proof of it!

I picked up an injury at Liverpool and that was the fairy tale pretty much over. I keep saying it but Sheffield United was a top club, no, is a top club and I was really lucky to get a chance to play there and be a part of something that was really special. I will never forget Leeds as I say, and the last game of the season v Crystal Palace when we went on the pitch at the end of the game with families, the civic reception, the whole lot. Fantastic memories.

My only regret was that I didn't get the chance to play more games alongside Chris Morgan. 'Morgs' is a top bloke and a great professional. He also became a great friend and I still speak to him a lot, as I do many of the Blades team which I was a part of.

I would like to think that we were very similar players, so maybe Warnock wouldn't have fancied unleashing the pair of us too often in tandem – who knows!

I am assistant manager now at Fleetwood with my old teammate and friend Graham Alexander. He had a late Premier League debut with Burnley as well and was still really enjoying the game. I had a spell with Southampton after leaving the Lane before a spell back with the Terriers, but Bramall Lane will always be special to me.

I am sure they all say it, but thanks to the fans that made me so welcome for the time I was there. The new investment looks exciting and I really hope you can kick on and get this proud and historic club back where it should be.

FOOTNOTE

For years I have walked out of the tunnel in front of the teams. It's a privilege and something that I never ever get tired of doing. I saw 'Lucky' lead out against us many times as skipper of clubs such as Huddersfield and Preston, and we always exchanged pleasant banter as we had a mutual friend in the shape of Martin Smith.

He was always one of those lads who conducted himself really well, one of the old school of professional footballers, as well as being a fierce competitor out on the pitch. It was interesting that he compared himself to 'Morgs', and I cannot argue with that.

Every time we go out to look for a defender, fans will say 'we need another "Morgs"', but that is getting harder and harder as football just doesn't produce players of that ilk anymore. The game has changed and moved on, as has the stance of the officials who control it. As a result, it has, perhaps, become much more sanitized, to say the least.

Chris was a typical Warnock signing at the time, brought in to bolster the troops for promotion and add another out-and-out leader to the ranks, and he more than played his part. Chris Lucketti is yet another of the many who have come to Bramall Lane after superb careers elsewhere, played relatively few games for the Club and yet really taken the place and the fans to their hearts.

A spell at Scunthorpe alongside Graham Alexander was followed by a brief stab at managing former club Bury, one that ended surprisingly after only a handful of games. At the time of writing the pair have just become the management duo at Salford City – a Club not yet in the League but most definitely on the up, and their arrival after successful spells at Highbury and Glandford Park has raised a few eyebrows. We wish him well; he did the job here that he was bought to do and made a lot of friends on the staff as he did it.

JAMIE WARD

A WARD-WINNING PLAYER

Jamie Ward set a record for the Blades at Wembley that he probably would sooner not have done! He spoke with me for the UTB programme article a few years ago to look back over his time at the Lane and his time as a Blade...

I had been at Chesterfield for a while and, to be fair, enjoyed the experience. They had signed me from Villa where I had been from being a youngster, and all had made me feel really at home, but my performances had brought me to the attention of quite a few clubs. Sheffield United were mentioned consistently as being one of those and it seemed fate when, in the transfer window, the Blades came calling. It was the original no brainer – near to where I lived and a Club with real passion, fire and tradition. I signed for Kevin Blackwell's side and we were well placed looking good for promotion.

The first thing I recall is the quality of players that we had at the Club – the dressing room was incredible and despite the fact that I have never been what you would call shy, it was a touch daunting the first time I walked into the training ground at Shirecliffe. This was a Premier League club in all but the division and I was ready to play a part in getting us there!

There was such strength of character and personality – 'Morgs' and Paddy to name but two, and I was made welcome from the off, and that is really important for a young player, it eases that transition and makes taking that step up much easier.

As history shows, we finished that season third in the table and that meant if we were going to do the business then it would be in the play-offs. I know that down the years for the Blades fans, this way is a real monkey on their back – fortune hasn't always favored the Club and as players we felt that we should have done it automatically, but that said we felt as a team that this would be our year. Of course, we got there, and the opponents were Burnley.

I never get over confident – a bit of nerves where football is concerned is never, in my book, a bad thing at all. That said, I didn't see us doing anything other than walking up the steps to collect the trophy. I knew I would be sub on the day but felt that if needed and called upon I could play my part in getting the Club back to where, in my opinion, it should be now – the Premier League.

We had had previous with the referee – not that there should be any difference in how that influences things, but I still feel we had a bad un. I was sent off late on for two handballs – one was fair enough but the second was never intentional. I became the first player in Sheffield United history to be sent off in a Wembley Final, not an accolade that I wanted. I was seething, and the Final whistle resulted in Lee Hendry also joining me on the naughty bench after the game had finished – not a day that I ended up wanting to remember. I mean, it's bad enough for a player, but I have always been tuned into fans and their emotions. I love the game, and Blades are brilliant. I felt that I had let everyone down – awful.

The following season I had scored four in seven and was on fire. The enemy from across the city came to Bramall Lane and I had never played in an atmosphere like that, even at Wembley, it was electric. The Sheffield derby is something unique. Someone said that it is the nearest it comes to an old firm game without religion being involved, but in the Steel City it means just as much, it's powerful.

I was lucky enough to score and what a moment that was. I was also unlucky enough to get injured. I did a hamstring over towards the John Street stand side of the stadium and that was my involvement over for the day, and for quite a few weeks. I don't know whose idea it had been to take me on the stretcher round in front of the visiting fans. I suppose it was the quickest way in terms of getting me treatment. They made it clear how much they thought of my contribution and goal celebrations. I wish I could have got off the stretcher to collect the pound coins that were getting launched, that would have been handy to go with the goal bonus! They still remember that I was a Blade and proud to be one when I have played at their place with the Rams. They give me a special welcome and it is always a pleasure to do well there to repay their support!

Eventually Gary Speed took over the reins from Blackwell and I can honestly say that he is one of the greatest people I have ever had the privilege to know, let alone play with. I was in awe of a man that I grew up as a football fan watching on *Match of the Day* – a class act on and off the field.

I don't mind telling you that when he became Boss he had me in the office and asked if I was on a bonus for goals scored. I told him I was, not uncommon for a forward. He then asked if I was on the same for assists. I had never heard anything like that and told him it wasn't the case. He then said that I was, from that moment, on an official bonus; however, 'Speedo' was paying the bonus from his own pocket – no worries there. I was stunned, but that is the sort of person he was – amazing.

My blood ran cold when I heard that he was dead. He had gone out of his way to help me and others and had always put an arm around me. I was in bits after Wembley and it was Gary who told me not to worry, there would be other chances and my dismissal hadn't really been the be all and end all on a bad day at the office.

I think I was one of the first to come down and lay some flowers at the Lane in front of the statues. On reflection, it was such a futile gesture – I don't know what I thought would come from it, but I just wanted to say how I felt. I have never got over the fact that he isn't there any more, at the other end of a phone for a chat or support. Selfish of me I suppose, but he was a big influence.

When 'Speedo' went and Micky Adams came in, I knew my days would be numbered. I had two great years or thereabouts at the Lane, although I was plagued by injury and I still don't think that the fans ever saw the best of me in my time there, and that is a personal disappointment. The club wanted to move me on and Derby came in. I can honestly say that the fans have been great, and the manager has really been good to me at Pride Park, but, as many former teammates have often said, wherever you go when you leave the Lane there is always a piece of Sheffield United that stays in your heart. I made some great friends there who I still stay in touch with: 'Monty', 'Kozzy' and many others, as well as staff behind the scenes.

I just want to thank the fans for their support whilst I was there, it was an honour to have been a part of things at Sheffield United and I wish it could have ended on a better note for all. Although most of the players from my time have gone, I still always look for the result and I think that, from what I hear, things could be taking a turn for the better at last in S2. I hope that United get back this season. I will be across to watch a game or two when fixtures allow.

FOOTNOTE

As Jamie said, he was one of the first people in the car park that terrible day at Bramall Lane when the news came out that Gary Speed had taken his own life. Dave McCarthy and myself had headed into the stadium as we both knew that fans and the general public would instinctively head there as they felt they wanted to lay a tribute in his memory. In terms of his football career, 'Speedo' had spent less time with us than anyone, but he had left his mark on all that he dealt with or he met – a true professional and a really top man, as the tributes laid around the statues over the days that followed gave testimony to.

Jamie has stayed in touch wherever he has played. Nigel Clough had him at Derby and they got on well. We were all surprised that 'Wardy' never made a return to the red and white stripes under his tenure. He became one of the few to play for both Derby and Forest and be accepted by both sets of fans, and he also had a spell with Clough on loan at Burton. He turned up at Bramall Lane with Cardiff City on their hunt from promotion under Neil Warnock in the 2017-18 season, again on loan and looking to secure a permanent deal. They went up so let's hope he was successful.

MARTIN SMITH

SON OF?

Many will recall that, although Adrian Heath had an ill-fated spell as our Manager, his eye for talent at a bargain price was formidable to say the least. In his brief tenure he brought in players such as Marcus Bent from Port Vale, Bruno Ribeiro from Leeds United, Shaun Murphy from West Brom and Martin Smith from Sunderland. Although Smith's tenure was a short one, he left his mark. We take up his story from a UTB interview from 2015…

I began my career as a youngster with Sunderland, the Club I supported as a kid. I loved it at Roker Park and also played for England at Schoolboy and Youth International level. I got a cap for the Under-21s as well, so all was very good very early. I made me League debut for the Black Cats against Luton Town in late 1993 and marked the event by scoring – real *Roy of the Rovers* stuff for a lifelong Mackem, I can tell you that!

I played quite frequently in the first couple of seasons and had a great relationship with the Roker faithful – they nicknamed me 'Son of Pele' – no pressure there then! I slipped down the pecking order a bit and then also fell fowl of injury to a degree. There came a point when it was quite clear that to develop my career I was going to have to get away and start again – but that is football and you take the rough very much with the smooth.

I declined a new deal and joined Sheffield United. Adrian Heath had just taken the hot seat from Steve Bruce and was looking to change things and freshen them up. There were some cracking players there: Paul Devlin, Curtis Woodhouse and Wayne Quinn to name but three. I had worked with 'Inchy' at Sunderland and liked and respected him. He had just really finished as a player. He had a spell at United under Howard Kendall, and I liked his ideas and plans. I signed for a year. I had lost my way and knew that – the deal gave me a chance to show that I could go for it – the understanding with me and the manager was that if I could show the form that I had once promised the deal

could be re-negotiated accordingly. I was getting the chance at a big Club and was fired up.

I moved to the area. We bought a place at Holmfirth, and I couldn't wait to get started. Adrian's time at the Lane wasn't the best for him – results were not going his way and as Christmas loomed we looked in big trouble at the foot of the table. It was a real shame, he had an eye for a bargain and brought players like Marcus Bent in from Port Vale for about £300,000 – a real bargain – as well as Shaun Murphy and quite a few others. He also got Riberio in from Leeds – he could play a bit as well – something just didn't click.

I came on for my debut as a sub in the League Cup and got a brace. Quite quickly I seemed to build up a good relationship with the fans. I loved the Club and settled very quickly into life here. I tended to drop just in behind the front two and play as an attacking midfielder, and that suited me down to the ground. We also tried to play football and that was crucial as well.

I will never forget going up to St James' Park for a cup game v Newcastle. They knew who I was and my love of all things Sunderland and natural dislike of all things Magpie, so it was fantastic to score for the Blades in front of the Gallowgate end of the ground and reel away with my finger to my lips to silence the stick I had been getting from the off. I would never have to buy a beer in the Washington Working Men's Club for the rest of my life!

Our fans were in the top corner of the stand and a few of them were also at the other side at the very front towards the Leazes' Park End of the stadium. I think they had to allow more tickets than usual because of regulations so it was difficult for the Blades to make any real noise and we got drowned out, which was a shame. I was gutted we lost. I always remember going to see a young lad called Ben Laylor – a Blade who was recovering from a multiple transplant in hospital up there. What a brave lad he was, certainly put things into perspective I can tell you.

Adrian was replaced by Neil Warnock. A great manager, but I knew that I would not be his type of player, as wouldn't Bruno. It was just one of those things really. I had already got contract discussions penciled in, and I had to knock on the new Manager's door to have a look at what could be done. I was quite surprised when he offered me a deal; that said, it was substantially less than Adrian had offered, and I was a bit disappointed. I had shown good form and finished with 12 goals in my first 17 games, had been injury free and had really got a taste for it all.

The rejuvenation had also put me back in the shop window and others were, knowing I had only signed a fairly short-term deal, sniffing around me and United. When I say I signed for a low wage I mean it in relative terms – a professional player earns far more than the working man and I have always respected that as I come from a real working-class background. I only asked for a bit more than was on the table at that point. Neil stuck to his guns and I have to applaud that.

Huddersfield Town, managed ironically by Steve Bruce, came in with a £300,000 bid – not too bad a profit on a player who had signed for free and scored a fair few goals. The Terriers were having a real go in terms of players and ambition, although I would really have loved to have stayed, the Clubs agreed a fee and I was on my way to the Galpharm.

I really mean this – I loved United. Great ground, city and fans. The staff at the Lane were also the very best and I still keep in contact with John Garrett. I came back for the 125 game v Wolves last year and went for a beer after in the Cricketers with JG. I didn't think anyone would remember me let alone want to talk. I was touched by the handshakes, requests for photographs and the overall warm welcome I got.

When a career is over you cherish things like that, you really do, and in the darker times, when you miss the craic of the dressing rooms and the banter that is unique to the game, those are the things that carry you through. I am still in the game – I work as an agent in the North East and watch games up there. It was only a short time, but I am proud of my time as a Blade – I have a big picture of me scoring in front of the Kop that takes pride of place at home.

Thanks to all of you who said hello and reminded me of happy times in the pub that afternoon. A great club and great people – I know it has been said many times but once a Blade definitely always one.

Good luck to all at the Lane – let's hope Nigel Clough can get The Blades back where it belongs. When he does there will be no one more delighted, you all deserve it.

FOOTNOTE

When you work in football, there are players that you will get on with like a house on fire whilst they are here, then when they leave you will never see or hear from them again. There are those that you just don't gel with and the feeling is very much reciprocated, and ones that are firm friends whilst a player and stay in contact with you long after they have left – Martin Smith is definitely one of those.

He went to Huddersfield as one of Steve Bruce's first real signings and picked up a nasty injury that put him out of the game for a while. He rang me one Christmas morning on his way into training and rehab, down and depressed that he thought he wasn't going to make it back – one of those moments that I suppose all pros in the same circumstances go through at times, when all the rest of the world seems to be happy and celebrating.

He was ready for packing it all in but managed to come back and ended up with a move to Northampton Town who, at that point, were having a real go and offering more than potential suitors in the Championship, such as Rotherham and Forest. In the end, injuries beat this talented player as a pro, though he turned out for Blyth Spartans in Non-League for a time a bit nearer home in Sunderland. Martin is now a player agent and still a good mate who attends games at Bramall Lane a couple of times each season.

CHRIS ARMSTRONG

AT FULL STRETCH

Chris became a Blade following a transfer from Oldham Athletic in 2003. On the wanted list of many clubs, he went through many ups and downs at the Lane but won the respect of all Blades for his determination and refusal to quit in the face of adversity. 'Stretch' takes up the story…

When I joined the Blades from Oldham there were a few other clubs looking at me. I had a great time at Boundary Park but they were in a few difficulties financially, so a decent offer was always going to be hard to turn down.

I knew that United were interested before the end of the 'Triple Assault Season', so I began to watch games and results with interest, particularly the game v Wolves at Cardiff. The result didn't go our way, but the support at the ground and the excitement they generated convinced me that my future was as a Blade.

Neil Warnock was regrouping, and I came around the same time as 'Morgs'. The first thing that struck me was the sheer size of the City of Sheffield – huge – and Bramall Lane. I am not kidding, but when I first walked out on that pitch in a game I found it a little daunting if I am being honest, but I soon settled in.

Sheffield United are a very warm club and they went out of their way to get me settled in and did a great job. Neil Warnock was a great man-manager to play for and he knew how to put an arm around a player, and that was a big help, a very big help indeed.

What a great dressing room that was – it had that unique balance between the young players such as me, 'Tongy', 'Jags', 'Monty' and the older, more seasoned professionals that were there to guide and advise. Stuart McCall was also brilliant to be around. The thing was that, although all happy and goods friends, we all had ambition. We knew where we wanted to go and were prepared to graft to get to where we needed to be. The training ground was a great place – welcoming and hard working.

I remember playing a pre-season game v 'Boro' and being turned inside out by Juninho – that's never good when 'Boro' fans know that your football allegiances lie elsewhere in the North East by the way! My League debut was against Gillingham and it was memorable for being boiling hot and not a lot else, it wasn't one for the purists.

I settled well, and the first 15 games were OK, then I did my knee away at Ipswich Town fairly late on in the game. A fairly robust challenge saw the gaffer and Macca going berserk on the touchline. I knew it was serious and I heard it go – that was the start of one of the hardest 18 months of my life. My brother Gordon was a long-time professional and I leaned on him for help and advice.

I had three ops in the next year or so – it was a bleak time for a young lad who just wanted to play football, and I was determined to get back. One of the leading specialists advised me that it would be a good idea to call it a day and retire, and I don't mind telling you that I was numb at the very thought. I decided to go through with one last operation – real make or break stuff. Thankfully that proved successful and, against all of the odds, I got back to fitness – I had to prove them wrong.

By the time I got my next chance of the first team, we were already 15 or 20 games in and the spirit in the camp was second to none. That was a brilliant season – I played again and we were promoted – one of the best years of my life, it was wonderful, and I will never forget it.

It was Kevin Blackwell who sold me to Reading. I don't think that he was my biggest fan and the competition for a shirt was huge. After all I had been through I wanted to play as much football as possible and the Royals had just been relegated and was a top set-up – it was a good move at the time but one that I didn't want. I loved Sheffield and was very happy at the Club, but that is football and you take your chances when they come around.

It was there that I was diagnosed with MS and, as a result, ended my playing career. I haven't had an attack for four years now and I work hard on doing the right things and keeping as fit as I possibly can. I keep healthy and take the time to really enjoy my family – priorities have now changed. I take a bit longer to recover and come around then I used to do. I was invited to the 125 celebrations the other week and I would have loved to have been there and seen the lads and the fans and staff, but I had been in Ireland the week before and was genuinely struggling. I left it to the day before but had to drop out and that was sad for me.

I watch plenty of football and always look for our results first. My nephew is the Captain of Hull City's reserves, so it will be an interesting day on April 13th in our family, though there will be only one team I will be cheering, and I hope to be at the Lane very soon!

FOOTNOTE

It's easy to forget the horrendous injury that he overcame to play again – I recall how hard he worked in the gym and with the medical and physio staff to get back, and at the time it was inspirational to see him – dedicated and determined but without ever losing his sense of humor. He was resolute that he would be back and playing as soon as was possible.

The fans of Reading took him to their hearts as well when he joined them from the Blades. He came back here as guest of honor when we played them and was presented with a shirt from both clubs as a mark of respect for the service he had given. The fact that, as a player, he was struck down with MS really illustrates that even in the glamorous life of a professional football player, such a tragic illness can strike. It ended his career – one that he had fought hard to keep alive.

I expected him to be a changed man, such things and their effects on you and your family are hard to imagine, but it hasn't changed him at all. His is active, runs marathons and has even played at a decent level in Non-League Football.

There is no change in Chris in terms of determination and humor. He has visited Bramall Lane on quite a few occasions since this was written as our guest for games and he is always welcome. Young footballers and the world in general could learn a lot from the attitude and steel of Chris Armstrong.

DAVID FRAIN

LOCAL AND LOVED IT

There have been a few down the years who have 'lived the dream' – local lads and fans who have managed to pull on the shirt and play for the Blades. 'Frainy' was one who did just that, and also went on to carve out a good career as a pro. He still lives in area in which he grew up and attends games on a regular basis. I spoke with him in 2015 about his career and the memories it brings back...

I was born in Heeley to a family of Blades and grew up very much as one of them. Bramall Lane was like a second home. I played football at school and also turned out on a Saturday for Dronfield Town, which was a decent standard and, as a result, I had a fair few clubs keeping an eye on me. I signed schoolboy for Forest when Brian Clough was Manager, but I was released after two years – it was just one of those things.

Now, the Sheffield United connection and how it worked... I used to play on a Sunday for Rowlinson who had a pretty good side back then. The manager was Derek Dooley and I got on with him really well. When he knew I was available he managed to organise a six-week trial when Ian Porterfield was the manager. Derek was a big influence in my life, along with Danny Begara, but more on Danny later.

I did well enough during my trial to be offered a year. What a dream come true. Sunday football to a chance with the team I loved back then and still do. One of the other lads told me to ask for a signing-on fee. I was working as an apprentice electrician at the time and he said to tell the manager that it would give me added security as I would be quitting a steady job.

To be honest, I would have played for United for nothing, I was that excited. He told me to ask for five grand – I had never even thought of that sort of money – back in 1985 that was a colossal amount and it scared me to death.

Ian Porterfield offered me £150 per week for a year. I was on £112 in my job, so that was a massive increase over what I was on, but that was

immaterial. I bottled it – when I asked for a signing-on fee the manager said that he would have to ask the chairman, who at that time was Reg Brearley – he was away in India. When he asked how much I just said five hundred quid – he just said that he didn't think that would be a problem!

That came back to bite me. At the end of my 12 months I got another two years and a pay increase. I was also due another signing on fee and it could not be less than my last one – you got it, another £500. I signed away ten grand in a year!

I scored on my debut v Sunderland. There I was playing in the same team as Keith Edwards, Paul Stancliffe, Colin Morris – heroes. How much would Keith be worth today? A player with that God-given talent should never have to work again.

Playing for the Club didn't worry me, it was the Sheffield thing that weighed heavily on your shoulders. If you had a bad game, family members told you, mates told you, you got it in the pub on a Sunday, on the bus, shopping in town... It is never the Sheffield way to hold back on opinion is it?

I would have given an arm to play for the Blades, but I didn't really begin to develop as a player until I went to Rochdale. I played Dave Bassett's first game as manager and I thought I did quite well. I will always like and respect him; he took me on one side and told me that he didn't think that my style of play would fit – fair enough – he also said that he could fit me up with a Club in Sweden, but I didn't want to go abroad. It was then that Danny Begara changed my life by taking me to Rochdale.

What a man. The thing with Danny was that he was so far ahead of his time as a coach; he also could do everything he preached and more. One of his party pieces was to get a ten-pence piece out of his pocket, flick it from his toe to his shoulder, down his arm, the back of his neck etc faultlessly before finally flicking it back into his pocket. Brilliant.

Now it became a bit more like a normal job. I played for the Dale, enjoyed it and then went home. Family and friends weren't watching and offering their critique. I found it more enjoyable – a lot easier – and, as a result, swept the board at the Player of the Year awards in my first season.

Had it not been for a bit of a language barrier at times, I genuinely think he could have been a top, top coach. I had three great years with the Dale and have only the very best of memories of my time there

I followed him to Stockport County and, again, we had a fantastic time there — in fact, one of the best in their history. Danny is still celebrated there and quite right too. I Captained the Hatters at Wembley twice out of four appearances. In fact, I was skipper at Edgeley Park for four of the years that I played there. I will admit that one of the reasons that I will not watch the Blades at Wembley is the fact that I lost there as a player so many times and I consider myself as bad luck!

I ended up at Stockport by accident. I was originally off to play for Colin Morris at Scarborough before I bumped into Brendan Elwood in Sheffield.

He was Stockport Chairman and he talked me into the move – what a great stroke of luck that was!

I never fell out with Danny, but we had a bit of a stand off on a few issues and I was allowed to go out on loan for a spell to Mansfield Town. I did well there, and we even beat Leeds United at Elland Road in one of the cups. Andy King was the gaffer. Danny got a bit awkward about the fee and wanted my signing-on fee back as a part of it – a deal couldn't be reached and I returned. It was just one of those things, I never had hard feelings, Danny had been good to me and I always considered myself as fortunate to have had a chance in the first place.

After a short spell in Hong Kong, I came home and played Non-League Stalybridge Celtic, Alfreton etc before packing in. I now work as an electrician for Morrison's and am based in Leeds most of the time. As a result, I don't get to as many games as I would like, but I am there when I can.

Before the game against Chesterfield I went in the pub for a few beers and I love talking about the players, the game and the Club. The best part of all that is that I got to do it for real – thanks to Derek Dooley I played for Sheffield United. I had the chance that many will only ever dream of – I pulled on the shirt – I played for the Club that I love, and for that I count myself very fortunate.

I think this is our year – good luck to the lads and Nigel Clough.

FOOTNOTE

'Frainy' really is the best example you could get of never knowing who you are stood next to in a pub. He lives a walk away from Bramall Lane and loves nothing better than to have a few quiet beers with his mates before walking down to the ground to cheer the Blades on, yet unless you know him you would never know that he had been a player. He is a great lad, quiet and unassuming, and never lets on about the career that he once had and the time he was a player for the Blades unless you push him.

It is also interesting that he places the great Derek Dooley so high up in his list of influences. You never hear a bad word about 'Del', and quite rightly so – the father figure of so many players and staff at Bramall Lane and one that so many turned to for advice. I suppose the fact that he came from the streets of Sheffield and made it to the top, first as a player and then as a manager and administrator in football, meant that he had a wealth of experience and knowledge of both life and the game that could be readily tapped in to, and the advice and arm around the shoulder was always freely given if needed.

David Frain did what I suspect every one of us would kill to do – he played for the Blades, and that gave him memories that no money could ever buy.

MICHAEL BROWN

OH LORD!

At the time of this interview, Michael Brown was moving towards playing in the EFL at the age of 40, well over a decade after leaving the Blades, in a career that had seen him play for Spurs, Fulham, Portsmouth, Wigan and Leeds United after kicking it all off with Manchester City.

'Browny' lined up against the Blades for Port Vale on Boxing Day and had his name read out to a standing ovation from the travelling fans. UTB found out that the admiration and respect is very much mutual as we caught up with our former midfield star early in the New Year...

To be honest I doubt things have ever got much better in terms of how I felt and the memories it evokes than being stood on the balcony of the Town Hall in Sheffield looking out over the thousands of fans who had turned out to salute

the team for a season that had inevitably produced nothing and yet promised so much. I mean, if United could just take the next step, still the possibilities are limitless. The Blades are a huge Club and I am so proud that I have been one of those fortunate to play for them, but let's start at the beginning…

I am a Hartlepool lad and I attended trials with many clubs before I was eventually signed by Manchester City. Plenty wanted me, but they handed out the offer of the longest contract and the Club felt right to both me and my Dad, so it was to Maine Road that I went and to a Club totally unrecognisable to the one that carries the name today.

I was signed by Peter Reid as a youngster but given my chance by Alan Ball. He was a top bloke and I think I was, at that time, one of the youngest-ever Premier League debuts at the age of 17.

I have been fortunate to see football from every division and was lucky even to spend some time at home-town club Hartlepool on loan. City was a great club with some big players. I remember Nigel Clough when he came from Liverpool – Nigel was some player and no mistake. Always quiet and he kept himself to himself – there was even rumors going around that he occasionally smiled from time to time! It is no surprise that he has become a quality manager – he has something different in his locker, that extra something, and he will do big things for the Blades.

Despite being involved in the Play-off Final victory over Gillingham, Joe Royal had made it clear that I would not be featuring in his plans. Alan Ball again came to my rescue and took me to Portsmouth on loan. He made it clear that it was just for a month and it became obvious when I got there. They were in a hell of a mess, but it had got me some first-team action. I played against United at Bramall Lane and Neil Warnock got downwind of me – again. He said that there was no chance of a permanent move as the Club were skint, but as we improved so did the crowds and income. Manchester City agreed to let me go for a realistic fee of around £375,000 and let United pay it over the term of the contract, which was a big help, so I became a Blade.

It wasn't a bad team: Simon Tracey, Wayne Quinn and even Bobby Ford were decent, and we also had Marcus Bent and a few others, as well as 'Jags', 'Monty' and 'Tongy' coming through. Warnock built and changed things steadily

– nothing happened overnight, and a lot of lessons can be learned in football from that ethos today. The changes, over a period of time, were incredible – we went from Abbeydale where we got changed in an old cricket pavilion, to a state of the art complex at Shirecliffe, but what never diminished was the closeness of the players and staff.

You raced to get in to the Club every morning for your tea and toast before training because the banter and spirit was just that good – easily the best I have ever known. The thing about United was that we all helped each other out – you could always ask a favour, whether it was from Emma Wylie in the Ticket Office or the Manager – people would go out of their way to help and that is so special, believe me, other clubs aren't like Sheffield United behind the scenes. It is a family and that's what helped make us the Club we were back then. We laughed and laughed and did everything with a smile. A real team.

Neil got the right balance. Stuart McCall came to us at the back end of his career and made it easy for me, 'Monty' and 'Tongy' in particular. It seems these days that older players aren't wanted – I am lucky to be with a Club and hopefully making a difference, but 'Macca' made us tick. 'Pagey' was class – Paddy is one of the best keepers I have ever played with – 'Jags' was brilliant. Sometimes it is just right isn't it?

Back to the Town Hall balcony – 2002/03 – we didn't get what we deserved. That run of games was incredible and gave me memories that will never ever leave me. We just should have walked away with something to show for it. Forest was the best game I have ever played in at home, and I remember the stick I took at the City ground for the foul and subsequent penalty I tucked away in front of the West Bridgford End – our fans were in the lower tier. It is as clear as the penalty I missed in the Play-off Final at Cardiff, but for very different reasons of course. So near yet so far, but it lit the fuse for the return to the Premier League a couple of years later.

I didn't want to leave United, but I wanted to play at the highest level as every footballer should. I could have gone to Glasgow Rangers and Liverpool over the course of that summer, but still wanted to go again with the lads. As we approached Christmas, results hadn't perhaps matched the season before and the opportunity to join Spurs was too good at the time to turn down – I could have signed a pre-contract agreement that would have seen the Club get nothing as I moved under freedom of contract the following summer, but I didn't want to do that. United got £750,000 for me and I am sure that helped out.

Spurs were different. Daniel Levy has done a great job there. It was private planes to games, special chefs and the very best of everything. I loved my time there, but it wasn't United. I really mean that.

I love Sheffield United and I always will, but I promise you that many ex-players will say the same on the back of their time at Bramall Lane. I could have come back on several occasions. Terry Robinson rang me literally minutes after I had agreed terms with Wigan – I was on my way to tie everything up, otherwise I would have been back. They always say that you should never go back, but it would have been a no-brainer for me. Such is life – it would have been great but that is how it sometimes goes.

I was at the Play-off Finals as a fan and felt the same pain as everyone else when we failed to get back – it meant the world on Boxing Day when I got the reception I received from the Blades behind the goal, and I hope that I can play some part when Vale play at the Lane. It is my ambition to make a Football League appearance when I am 40 – I have a £1 bet with my best mate and I intend to collect it!

I keep in contact with everyone at United from my time there and am immensely proud that I have served the Club – it was and always will be one of the best times of my life. I will be there when Spurs are the visitors, along with 'Kozzy', cheering us on. UTB!

FOOTNOTE

The passing of time saw 'Browny' take the reigns as manager of Vale as Rob Page moved on to Northampton. To keep the Blades tradition, he took Chris Morgan and David Kelly as coaches, but it would end in disappointment when they parted company with the Club after a string of poor results. Sharp as a tack, he has begun to make his mark as a pundit for television, and very good he is too. Regardless of any of his other former clubs, he has always had a real soft spot for the Blades. Derek Dooley signed him after a period on loan for £450,000 and said it was one of the best deals that he ever did in football. Bernard Halford, stalwart of Manchester City, allowed him to join and said he was too cheap. Derek knew the lad needed a fresh start and Bramall Lane was the ideal place for it to happen. It has to be said that the players of that time were a top bunch of lads. Neil was excellent at picking good characters and, as a result, most of them are still in touch today. 'Kozzy' was his scourge and the pranks he pulled on his mate were legendary – the soles of Browny's Gucci shoes were still visible on the first-team dressing room floor until recently after being glued there in 2003!

BRIAN HOWARD

SOMETIMES IT DOESN'T FIT

We caught up with former midfielder Brian Howard as he landed back in the country after a spell abroad to sign for Birmingham City. A lad who has always kept in touch with staff at the Lane, we asked him about his time here and the controversial switch across from Oakwell back in 2014...

I was very lucky at Barnsley – a Southern lad moving up to the People's Republic of South Yorkshire and being accepted was quite an achievement. I helped play a big part in the FA Cup run that year – we lost out to my former club Chelsea, but it was a hell of a ride.

We had been good for each other, but I had decided that if I was going to take the career a stage further then a move was the solution. When I made it clear I wanted to leave, the fans were upset, and I don't blame them for that. Wolves were showing interest but when Sheffield United came in, as far as I was concerned it was the original no brainer.

After meeting Kevin Blackwell, the deal was very much done – as the window had closed I agreed to initially join on loan with a fee agreed for when transfer activity could start up again, and I joined in October 2008. The dressing room was full of big players – no disrespect to the Reds, but in our dressing room there were players like 'Morgs', James Beattie, Ugo Ehiogu and Paddy Kenny.

Gary Speed was there as well, and what an honor that was to be in his company. He was a player that I had watched on television and admired from being young, and here I was sat next to him in the changing room. What a gentleman, I know that you interviewed Jamie Ward and he said the same thing, nothing was too much trouble and he was so genuine – what a loss.

One of the major advantages of joining the Blades was that I got to escape from the curse of Kozluk. I know he is a legend at the Lane for his humor and pranks – they were funny until it was you that was the brunt of things!

IN OTHER WORDS

I joined United because it was a team that was, in my opinion, going places and very fast indeed. You only had to look at the squad that was available to the Manager and it was easily one of the best outside of the top flight – in fact, I think that, on paper anyway, it was probably a hell of a lot better than many of those at the bottom end of the Premier League. I never had any doubts that we would go up – such was the strength.

The Lane was and is a great ground to play at – it didn't take me long to settle in – as I have said, it was a great bunch of lads and I learned a lot very quickly indeed. The way we did things here was very different. For a start the training ground and the way in which players worked and were looked after was a different class.

I recall when we went out on one of the Malta trips how well thought out things were. It was hot out there; in fact, I reckon at that time one of the hottest places I have ever been to play football. Such were the conditions that the Club doc and physio limited us to no more than 45 minutes out in the sun at any one time – we all went down is shifts. Apparently, it was due to the harmful effects of the UV light, so you live and you learn!

That season we really put ourselves in a truly great position to go up – it was in our hands, and it has to be said that we blew it. I scored in a 1-0 over Reading, which I think put us second – it was a 0-0 against Forest and a 0-0 against Palace, when we took magnificent support to Selhurst Park. The backing was unreal, but luck wasn't on our side for a change, so it was the play-offs – never good words around the Lane.

Preston in the Semis – and I thought we played really well over both games – the aggregate should have been bigger, but it was irrelevant, we got through to the Final at Wembley. Automatics are great, but you know what, if you had a choice and it was nailed on you would do it at the National Stadium in front of 20 or 30,000 of your fans – I would take that every time – there is something magical about the place and that will never change.

Other lads have also said this, but I never thought that we wouldn't beat Burnley, and I don't mean that in an over-confident way – I genuinely don't. We had a top side and I felt we would deliver on the day – repay our magnificent fans.

We should have gone up, but to do that you have to turn up, don't you? The reality was that we didn't – and in spectacular style. Add that to the madness of the Final minutes – the red cards – everything. It was a nightmare – all I could do was think of the fans and the backing they had given.

I read an interview with Clarke Carlisle, who was on the Burnley side that day – he said that, as far as he was concerned, we should have had two stone wall penalties, one for a foul on me, the other for one on Kyle Walker – I respect the honesty of someone I have always regarded as a top pro, but it will never change the history books, will it?

Going up would have silenced our critics – it would have silenced those who got on my back for leaving Barnsley. At the end of the day the only way to do that is by producing the goods, and it didn't happen. I often think how different it could all have been, where would Sheffield United be now? Where would mine and other careers have gone? All questions that will never be answered.

I have to be honest, the kind of system the manager employed didn't get the best out of me and players who liked the ball. In hindsight, I can't understand why he bought me, and I suspect that Leon Britton feels exactly the same – I loved it at United but I feel sad that the fans didn't see the best of me.

I moved to Reading – the manager was happy for me to stay but I needed to play the way I knew – I liked it there and remember coming back on a Tuesday night with the Royals – I think I got a decent welcome and there is no better place to play football on a night game under lights than Bramall Lane. It is a special place with a unique atmosphere. After a spell abroad, I have just signed for Birmingham City and am looking forward to being back in the Championship – we have to visit Hillsborough, so I will be looking up a few friends from United and trying to make sure that we walk away from there with all three points!

FOOTNOTE

Despite representing England at Under-21 level, he was deemed eligible to play for Scotland via his father's side of the family and called up by George Burley – a decision that was overturned by FIFA as they said that he had not been registered

early enough in his life. Brian fought to overturn it but to no avail. He went into Non-League Football and played latterly for Whitehawks in 2017, a Club that have attracted a fair few former league players into their ranks.

When I last spoke with him he was working as a Football Agent and watching games up and down the country, as is the nature of the job. It would be fair to agree with him – United never really saw the true potential of a player that had shone for Barnsley, particularly in that famous cup game v Chelsea. The Reds fans were angry that he left them, particularly as his choice of destination was Bramall Lane.

At that point he was definitely one of the players outside the top flight who stood out, and he was being courted by a number of clubs when he joined the Blades. Maybe it was the type of football here that didn't suit him, or the fact that the Club was beginning to head into a bit of a spiral that saw a need to clear the decks of some player wages, who knows?

What remains is, once again, a former player who loved his time in the Club and city and who keeps in touch with colleagues here without fail. One of many.

JOCK DODDS

GAME CHANGER

Some people change your life, and Jock Dodds was one of them. At the time of this early interview in 2002, he was the oldest surviving player to have appeared in an FA Cup Final – he turned out for the Blades v Arsenal in 1936 and was one of our greatest ever goalscorers and a real pre-war living Blades legend. I used to meet him in Blackpool at the behest of Kevin McCabe and Derek Dooley on a regular basis, and he would come over to Sheffield by train as our guest once or twice a season. He became like a surrogate grandad and could talk for hours about Sheffield United and football that was long gone in a sepia haze. He truly was the last of his kind...

I was born in Grangemouth in 1915 as the war raged. My father was killed in action. My mother re-married and we moved to Medomsley in County Durham. It wasn't long before I was playing football in the roads and parks of the area. I quickly progressed onto county schoolboys and then the local works team at Shell Mex – here I was a boy up against men, and I had to learn very quickly indeed.

I joined Huddersfield Town, initially as an apprentice, in 1932, signing professional terms in January 1933. It was a big thing that my family moved over there to support me. It was a fair old hike from where we lived on the outskirts to Leeds Road, and I used to walk there and back every day as another part of my regime – it was a good 10-mile round trip in all weather.

They were one of the best sides in the country back then – the legendary Herbert Chapman had not long since gone to Arsenal and it was a team of names. I struggled to get in and had a loan spell at Lincoln over that period of time.

It was also in this period that I read a book on the effects of eating meat and the effects that it could have on your health – cholesterol, blood pressure etc. – the question was posed asking why you would want to put dead carrion into your body – it painted a disgusting picture and I decided there and then never to eat meat again. The dog had everything in the pantry and I became

a vegetarian – there were not many of us back then – others thought I was a bit strange!

Teddy Davison signed me for Sheffield United after seeing me play my last reserve game for the Terriers. The huge Club that was the Blades were then in the old Division Two after being relegated out of the top flight of the English game the season before. A lot of famous names like Billy Gillespie and George Green had got old and retired, and Mr Davison was looking to rebuild and get them back up.

Moving to Sheffield was great – the family got a house on Kearsley Road next to the ground, so it wasn't far to go. Sheffield also had a fabulous culture – dance halls and such – it really was a big City and I loved the feel and buzz that it had. Magical.

I scored a hat trick in a reserve game and was given my first-team bow in September 1934 against Burnley in a 0-0 draw. I finally got my shooting boots on the following week away at Oldham – I scored one and I think 'Fanny' Barton got the other, and we still lost 3-2! His real name was Harold – not sure where he got the nickname from – he was a lovely lad from Liverpool and a cracking player.

Once Teddy Davison moved me from outside right to centre forward, it really began to happen. I was a big lad, strong, quick and I would also say brave. I could also look after myself and was never scared of an opponent – all of my seasons for Sheffield United from then on I finished as top goal scorer – my career record is one in two, or thereabouts.

1935/36 saw us get to the FA Cup Final for the sixth time in our history – I scored one of the goals in the game that saw the biggest crowd ever at Bramall Lane – over 68,000, against Leeds United in the FA Cup fifth Round. It was incredible, thousands of fans got onto the touchline on the cricket side when a gate in the corner of Shoreham Street and Cherry Street got forced about 20 minutes before kick-off. None of them would go out on the wicket as it was considered sacred!

The entire Wednesday team who had won the Cup in 1935 turned up that day to cheer us on – we knew them all and they were great lads. I scored against Spurs in the sixth round – I got a brace, and then we beat Fulham in the Semi-Final at Molineux.

It was a big deal for us to get there, believe it or not. We travelled down on the morning of the game by train. Tom Johnson, our Captain, got married to Gwen the day before and I was his best man! What a start that was. We walked out onto the pitch at Wembley and I really fancied us – we looked a right set in overcoats and hats – like the middle of winter!

I still think we should have won. I had a great chance. As I rose up to greet a Jack Pickering cross, Wilf Copping gave me a good nudge in the back and I just glanced it with my head instead of getting it full on. If I had there was only one place that it was going, and that was the back of the net! We lost 1-0 and I often wonder what could have been. I treasure my runner's-up medal, but my shirt was stolen not long after from my car on a visit back over the border.

We missed promotion narrowly that season – Manchester United were champions and Charlton runners-up, just three points in front. The Cup cost us, of that there was no doubt. As a treat, we went out on tour to Denmark, the first time Sheffield United had ever played abroad.

1938/39 saw two things happen. Firstly, United finally got back into the top flight of the game. Secondly, I realised that if I stayed at United I would never make any money. I was on 10 pounds a week – a lot of money for the time, but it would never change – as happy as I was I had to do something.

I knew that Joe Smith and Blackpool were interested in me. They had just bought Stan Mathews and needed to add to their attack. In those days, the Club held your registration even though you only got a contract that ran a year – this meant that even if they didn't offer you terms you still couldn't sign elsewhere unless they let you. Ridiculous.

I told Teddy Davison that I needed to go to a Club where the weather was better as the Sheffield smogs were affecting my mother's chest badly, which was true. I said that if a move could not be agreed then I would leave football at the end of a season and head for Canada to join the mounted police.

He was mortified. I was the leading goal scorer and he had just bought the wonderful Jimmy Hagan to play with me, but I was resolute. Blackpool, hearing this, came in with what I think was a record bid at that time of £10,000 for my services, and Sheffield United reluctantly accepted and I was allowed to meet them at the George Hotel near the railway station in Huddersfield, and it was here that I learned a very big lesson.

Joe Smith was a childhood hero of mine – he was some player at Bolton and had won three FA Cup-winner's medals with them – he told me that he wanted me and I was the missing piece of his jigsaw for the team he was building, which flattered me greatly. I asked him how much my wages would be a week and he told me it would be exactly the same as I was on at United – no change. I thanked him and said that, if that was the case, I would be staying at my Club until the end of the season then carrying out my idea of travelling to Canada.

I shook his hand, bid him farewell and made to leave.

'£1,000,' he said.

I turned and said, 'pardon?'

'Okay,' he said, '£2,000.'

I walked back – I genuinely didn't think I had heard him.

'Final offer – £3,500 to sign for us – take it or leave it.'

They were offering me a signing-on fee, the likes of which I could never have dreamed of. I also got wages that included win bonuses and even a few quid if the gate was over a certain number as well, alongside a place to live and a job for my mum. I left United and became, in effect, a rich man overnight. Crazy.

The Blades went up and were top of the League when war was declared, and the League abandoned. I played for other clubs such as Blackpool, Shamrock, Everton and Lincoln. I also had many adventures that one day, when I have gone, I am sure John will write about it, but I genuinely loved Sheffield United – what they have done to the ground now is fabulous – a credit to the owners.

I can't believe that, when I come back, people still want to meet me and ask for my autograph. I consider myself lucky to have played for such a great club, truly lucky.

FOOTNOTE

The longest piece for the oldest player. Trust me – he was a character. A formidable player, his scoring record is one of the very best of its time. A Scottish International who played in every war-time game, like many, he lost his best years to the conflict. He challenged the right of clubs to retain registration of players by arranging his own transfer from Blackpool to Shamrock Rovers – they took him to every court in the land along with the Football League, but he had done his homework and knew that the Irish club wasn't under their control and they couldn't touch him. He trained in Blackpool at the dog track, they flew him out on a Friday, he played, they paid him the colossal sum of £30 a game, then flew him back.

After six months his registration lapsed, and he signed for Everton. Queue more legal action that he won! He served time inside for selling re-labelled war-time dried milk to Blackpool holiday makers. He told me his solicitor advised him to plead guilty and he would get a slap on the wrist and a fine – he did and got 18 months! He famously said in the papers of the time:

'I thought I was a bit dodgy, but the judge was a joke!'

The middle man in the affair of the Bogota Bandits and a self-made millionaire, he was Bill Shankley's best man and Matt Busby's close mate.

You never met him without receiving a gift for the family. A box of chocolates for the missus, a toy for the kids, but you had to check the sell-by date on the chocolates!

To his last years, he was always wheeling and dealing. His last big deal was a consignment of thermal insoles for your shoes that made you taller and kept your feet warmer, I kid you not! He bought thousands on the cheap. Guess what you got for birthdays and Christmas after that? He gave Derek Dooley a pair once in the boardroom – Derek couldn't stop laughing.

I loved him to pieces. He is right, one day I will write the book, and it would make one hell of a film!

PETER DUFFIELD

BACK OF THE NET

Some of the best interviews that bring out the most fascinating stories are not from the more obvious former players. I caught up with Peter Duffield some five years ago to look back at his time at Bramall Lane, the trials and tribulations associated with that time and the memories that being a part of Bassett's boys conjure up today. 'Duff' takes over the story…

I had come through the ranks at my home-town club, Middlesbrough, at what was a trying time at Ayresome Park in the mid-80s. 'Boro' had a great squad back then with some superb home-grown talent such as Gary Pallister. The Club famously found the doors to the stadium padlocked shut as the receivers were called in. I recall the only people allowed to work were the groundstaff who were allowed to keep the playing surface tidy whilst the problems were sorted – I remember that we had two hours to get our kit out of the training ground – things really were that dire.

Danny Bergara had been my coach and, in the heat of the problems up there, he went back to Bramall Lane, where he had been such a success with Harry Haslam before. I had been an apprentice and found myself out of work and on the dole that summer, so I was glad that he remembered and liked me – that being the case he invited me for a trial at the then Billy McEwan-led Blades.

I was put up in a guest house at Hunters Bar – remember I wasn't being paid so I walked the distance to the stadium and back every day – I had no money so I couldn't afford dinner. The agreement with the place I was lodging and the Club meant that they were supposed to give me an evening meal – this they never did and neither did they try and make a lad a long way from home feel welcome, they didn't even talk to me.

I remember one night being sat in the lounge watching television when the woman who owned the place just came in and switched it off – it was about half past seven – unbelievable. I didn't say anything because I didn't want to be a problem, I just wanted a chance to get back in the game.

It was Peter Beagrie who found out that I wasn't eating and he sorted me out, made sure I was ok. 'Beags' was a top bloke, really funny and as mad as a hatter but with a real heart of gold and a great player. I bumped into him at a legends game a few years ago and he made a fuss. I owed him so much. When I needed it he put an arm around my shoulders and made me feel like I belonged, and I will never forget that.

Thankfully the Blades took me on, and for me it was the right time. Like now there was an onus on the manager to use younger players. They had just gone through the phase of having older, well-known names like Peter Withe and Ken McNaught – the money spent had changed the focus so Billy did just that. He is another that I will always be indebted to. I went from the dole to first-team football very quickly indeed.

I played in the first two games and by the time I had played 11 games I had scored seven goals. The team was in freefall though and Billy was sacked. History shows that Dave Bassett was brought in. 'Harry' famously says that he promised he would get the team out of the division – he did, we got relegated! Joking aside we were in trouble long before then. 'Harry' rebuilt – Beagrie was sold and others came in to get ready for a push.

The following season I was involved again. I think the number of subs went up – either way we started at Reading and we were off and running.

I weighed in with 15 goals – a bit-part player and 19 years old – what would I be worth now as a prospect? We had plenty of players who could weigh in with a few for us: Brian Deane, Tony Agana and Ian Bryson all knew where the back of the onion bag was didn't they? We all knew our jobs – there were no excuses where Bassett was concerned – a great team effort and work ethic was the key there.

When we went up I became a fringe player again, but when the chance arose I was there. It all came crashing down one Sunday morning game away at Swindon Town – I broke my leg in a challenge with Jon Gittens, although I scored from the result. It used to wind me up that, in some reports, he was credited with the goal!

There was an ambulance strike that day and there was only skeleton cover. It was just my luck that at the same time I went down seriously injured a fan in the stand had a fit and they had to deal with him first. I felt no pain whilst I was waiting to be taken to hospital – it was all down to shock. I recall the two stretcher men – one said to the other, 'it's bad – he will never play again.' 'Cheers', I thought!

That would turn out to be my Final league start for the Blades. I had massive complications with the break – the tib and fib fused, so I was out for a lot longer than was really expected at that time. The injury meant that when I finally came back I had to really change the way that I played football. I needed to accommodate the change of pace and, as a result, had to think a little bit more about the game as a whole.

I made some good friends at that time – Julian Winter, who is now chief executive, was struggling with a career-finishing injury at that time as well, so we spent a fair bit of time together as I came back slowly.

When fit, I was sent out on loan a few times. I really enjoyed Rotherham and managed five goals in 15 as they were relegated. I just wanted to play football.

Even though I spent six years over the border in Scotland and I am 'Boro born and bred, I regard Sheffield as my home, I love the city and I regard it as my home. Even though I still admit to being a lifelong Middlesbrough supporter, Sheffield United is a close second.

Everywhere we went our magnificent fans packed away ends all over the country, making every game just like one at Bramall Lane – they were and always have been different class –that's the difference between a genuinely big Club and one that plays at it.

I remember being told to warm up against Wolves and running up to the fans. The noise was so intense that I couldn't hear Geoff Taylor shouting us to come back – incredible!

My lad is a Blade and I am really proud of that, and the fact that I managed to play a small part in the success of that period.

I am still involved in the game as manager of Belper Town and I love it. That said, when I get the chance I am always back at the Lane and always will be. I love the place and let's just hope that we get back out of this division under Nigel Clough and his backroom staff – it's the very least this great club deserves.

FOOTNOTE

Since the interview, Pete has finished in football management – at least for the time being. For the last couple of seasons, he has worked as a matchday host for the Club, taking part in the sponsors meet and greet and tours before dining with and entertaining our guests. The thing with Pete is that he lives and breathes football. He also knows the game, so there can be few better dinner guests to have than 'Duff'. His passion for United really shines through. At times he is too modest – injuries often got in the way of playing more games. I recall being at Swindon on a Sunday in the 1989/90 promotion season when he scored a goal (some credited it as an OG for John Gittens) and broke his leg in the process. He was a brave little player and there can be no doubt of that. Wherever he plied his trade, he scored goals, and that is a rare commodity in the game. He still lives and works in the Sheffield area – another who settled in the Steel City that is proud of his time with the Blades – he is also a great lad!

TONY DAWS

WHEN DOORS OPEN...

Football can be a strange place at times. One cold Sunday morning at Rainbow Forge School, my lad's team lined up for a League game v local rivals Sheffield Spartans. On their touchline their Manager was former Blade Tony Daws, who a few short hours earlier had been in joint charge of a Scunthorpe side that had run out 2-1 winners at Fratton Park in front of 15,000 fans. I interviewed him later that week for the programme...

I was a local lad and a born-and-bred Blades fan. I went to Ashleigh School and was in the same year and school team as John Beresford, who went on to have a superb career with, amongst others, Portsmouth and Newcastle United.

I played for the Sheffield Boys team – we reached the Final of the FA Schools Cup or Gillette Trophy as it was known, and had a side that featured me, John, Darren Bradshaw and Frazer Digby. It was over two legs, with the first one at Bramall Lane and the second at Highfield Road. Sheffield won and my career was on its way. As a youngster I would ball boy at Blades games and I really loved it. I was in front of the Bramall Lane end when we played Sheffield Wednesday at Easter 1980. The score was 1-1 with McPhail weighing in for us and Curran scoring for the visitors. The atmosphere was electric.

I used to come down to the Lane a couple of nights a week and train in the cricket sheds, which were at the top of the Cherry Street car park with a lot of other young hopefuls at the time, but it was Notts County in the shape of Jimmy Sirrell and Howard Wilkinson who spotted something in me that they liked, and Notts County was the Club that I signed for.

I made my League debut there aged just 17 – it was away at Birmingham City and in their side were, amongst others, Mark Dennis and a keeper by the name of David Seaman, who went on to have a decent career, didn't he?

At all Clubs, Managers changed and the gaffer there didn't fancy me. My contract came to an end and I was on the lookout for another chance. Many will

tell you from my era that Danny Bergara was a big influence on them, and I was no different. As kids in the shed, he had taken a keen interest in me and, at the time, was head coach at Middlesbrough. He invited me up there; I had a look around and met the manager Bruce Rioch. All looked good and I was on the point of signing when he rang me and told me that it was on the verge of financially going belly up at Ayresome Park and that he was on his way back to Bramall Lane – the message was wait and join me there, which I did.

Imagine that. On a free and I get the chance to trial at my own Club – it was brilliant, and I put heart and soul into the opportunity. I joined United on the same day as Chris Wilder, he was another Sheffield lad and Blade through and through who got the chance as a youngster at Southampton, so I was in good company.

My break was given to me by Billy McEwan, and that is a story in itself. I got the chance against Blackburn Rovers on the Tuesday night at Bramall Lane in a reserve game. I thought I had played well and I got two goals against them. The manager must have also thought that I had been ok as we played in one of the cups the following day – I think it was the Full Members Cup, against Blackburn Rovers again and at Ewood Park – we lost that 1-0, and then again, on the Saturday, we played them at theirs in the League, won 2-0 and I got them both – incredible stuff!

There were a few thousand traveling Blades behind the net. For the first one I think it was Steve Wigley, who is now the assistant manager to Roy Hodgson in the England set up, who took the corner, Paul Stancliffe flicked it on and I nodded it into the net at the far post. The second goal came from a Peter Beagrie cross – real fairytale stuff for a young Blade - beats Jimmy Muir in *When Saturday Comes* doesn't it?

I started out up front with Peter Withe. There was a player who had been at the very highest level with Newcastle and Forest as well as winning the European Cup with Villa in 1982. The team also had, at first, one of my all-time heroes in the shape of Keith Edwards as well as John Burridge, Kevin Arnott, Martin Pike and many others – some great players.

That season I was in and out, which was no more than I expected with the competition being so high. I tried my very best all of the time – I remember getting the nod on Boxing Day 1986 against Hull City at Bramall Lane. It was a hell of a game – we won 4-2 and I scored with a volley at the Kop End – the perfect Christmas present and no mistake.

I had a year's contract and was gutted when they decided not to renew – it is all about opinion and I can tell you that I was on nothing in terms of wages. I was proud to play for my Club and I would have walked any distance to sign for them again. I was proud to pull on that red and white shirt – it meant the world – I really mean that.

I joined Scunthorpe from the Lane and have had some great times with the Club. I played the last season at the Old Showground and scored the first-ever goal at their new home, Glandford Park, in 1990/91. I was the fourth highest goal scorer in the country, just behind people like Steve Bull, with a respectable 27 in the back of the net.

I went to Grimsby and Lincoln City as well before I retired as a player. John Warnock contacted me in 1998 to see if I would be interested in working with the Under-9s at the SUFC Centre of Excellence and I jumped at the chance, progressing up to the Under-19s at a time when I also helped with the reserves alongside Neil Warnock and Kevin Blackwell – great times.

I was approached by Wednesday in 2004 to a more senior role in their set up, which for career progression I took, before becoming the head of the Scunthorpe Academy. I love Scunny and would do anything for the Club – at this point following the sacking of Brian Laws I'm in joint charge, though that will soon change, and I will go back to my day job!

I am still very much a Blade, live in Sheffield and also run my son's Sunday side – I just love the game!

FOOTNOTE

He is yet another local lad who played for the Club he had always supported, albeit for a brief spell. There can be no denying that there was some talent around Sheffield in the school's sides of the early 1980s – I remember Sheffield playing Coventry in that Gillette Final at the Lane and the players who were in it that went on to have good pro careers in the game very well. I think I am right in saying that we are one of the few cities that retained the trophy in consecutive years. The next batch had Carl Bradshaw and co.

There cannot be many former players of United who have lifted the prestigious Adidas Golden Boot: Steve Cammack did it, bizarrely also with Scunthorpe United and, of course, the great Keith Edwards got three – two with the Blades and one with Huddersfield Town, so Tony did pretty well.

I haven't seen him on a Sunday morning touchline for a while, but I wouldn't be surprised if he isn't still doing something at that level – he loves the game for what it is

STEVE CONROY

A SAFE PAIR OF HANDS

Another interview by phone was with former keeper Steve Conroy. Steve and his wife Shirley have a long history of running successful pubs over the years. He told of his time at Bramall Lane and the frustrations that both a succession of serious injuries and a monumental clash of personalities brought to his career. Over to Steve...

I was born in Chesterfield; in fact, I grew up in Staveley – a place that over the years had yielded some great Blades players. Joe Lievesley who played for the Blades and England in goal came from nearby Poolsbrook and the legendary Ernest 'Nudger' Needham came from Staveley as well.

I was scouted by another famous former player in the shape of Fred White, no mean keeper himself back in the day. When I signed for the Club I also had the chance to go to Arsenal, Spurs or West Bromwich Albion, all of whom were, and still are, great clubs. That said, and looking back, I was a little bit naïve in the sense that I had never really travelled that far from the place in which I grew up. I had played for North East Derbyshire, Chesterfield and England boys, but I had no real intention of moving too far away. Sheffield United were a top-flight club packed with great names, so the choice was easy.

It's hard to imagine, but whilst still not quite 16 years old I moved over to the City and I stayed in the residential house that the Club owned – it was called Moncrieffe House and it was in Nether Edge, not a million miles from the Lane. Even though I wasn't keen on leaving home, things there were ok - there were some other lads around at that time who were all good players, such as Tony Kenworthy, Simon Stainrod and, a little later, Keith Edwards. There was some good young talent even back then.

Alan Hodgkinson took an interest in my development and things went well. John Hope was in the first team at the time, although he suffered from dramatic drops in form. There was also Tom McAllister. Tom was a great keeper and had showed a lot of promise until his leg was broken in a challenge with Rodney

Marsh against Man City at Bramall Lane. Jim Brown, who was also a good stopper on his day, also came in.

I got my first sniff in the first team by accident. We were on tour at the end of the 1974/75 season and were due to play Al Shabab, a team in Kuwait. There was some issue with the stamps on a few of the party's passports, so Tom and a few others had to stay back in India. I was OK, so I went and I played. We won the game 2-1 and I did pretty well to be honest.

I had to wait until 1977, however, to get my league debut, and it was Jimmy Sirrell who gave me that. It was against Hull City on a Tuesday night at the Lane. We won 2-0 with goals from Keith Edwards and Bobby Campbell – again, I must have done alright as I kept the gloves for the next couple of games; in fact, I played five on the bounce.

The last of the sequence was away at Notts County in the old Anglo-Scottish Cup. Now County were the team that the manager had bossed before coming to Sheffield United and, to be fair, he is still regarded as something of a legend there. By my own admission I had an absolute mare and we lost the game 3-0. Sirrell made no secret that he blamed me for the result – he was under pressure from both the Blades fans and the board to deliver results. Add this to the fact that it was his old club and you get the picture – he wasn't a happy man. That game was on 6th September and he was relieved of his duties on 27th September, and that was the end of that, so to speak.

When Harry Haslam came in so did Danny Begara, and what a great coach Danny was. His methods took a bit of getting used to, especially for a goalkeeper, but he was brilliant. Danny wanted you to do things the continental way: that meant punching the ball out, and I had always been taught to handle the ball, kill it dead. It took a while for me to adjust, and during that time I had a few crises of confidence, but it was worth it. Danny was a top man.

I played pretty much all of the 1978/79 season as first choice. It was great to get the chance under Harry and I wanted to repay his faith in me, but we struggled and were, of course, relegated into Division Three for the first time in the history of the Club – bittersweet to say the very least.

Every time I got a break, I got a break in every sense of the word. A broken arm away at St Mirren in 1979 put me out for quite a while, then after I got back in I broke my collarbone, then I did my groin. finally, I fractured the pubic bone and that was the end of things, but that was much later on.

I was in goal that fateful day when Don Givens missed the penalty that would have kept us up – the Club needed change and Ian Porterfield was decided as the man to do it. I have never been one to hold back on what his opinion is, and neither was Porterfield. He was a terrific coach but difficult to get on with for me.

I had an interesting conversation with him when he first came in, then I went away on holiday. Whilst I was away he signed Keith Waugh. Back them 100 grand was big money for a keeper and as far as I was concerned you didn't pay that much to keep him in the reserves back then.

I went to see him, and he told me that I was still his first choice. I didn't believe him but you have to take things on face value, and we went away on tour. I played the first three games over the border against Clyde, Queen of the South and Ayr, losing the last one. Derek Richardson then played a few games before we kicked off the season against Hereford United – and it was Keith in goal.

Again, there was a heated exchange once more – he didn't like me and the feeling was fairly mutual at this point – me, Tony Kenworthy and John McPhail broke curfew – we were out of order and I knew it. All three were told to see the manager the following day – I was the only one there come the day of reckoning – the others were told not to bother. The manager even threatened to tell my wife that I had been out on the town – I couldn't believe it.

It got to the point where he wouldn't even play me in the reserves. I spent nearly two years having to attend reserve and junior games. I was made to write a report from the games in question just to prove that I had been there – I kid you not.

I wanted to get out and the response was, 'you can stay here and rot' – all I wanted to do was play. In the end I called the PFA in, I was owed a loyalty bonus and it was a fair amount of money – £10,000 – and the manager had refused to pay me. Gordon Taylor had a meeting with the Club and got a settlement. It was a lot less then I was due but it hopefully would bring things to an end. They also secured a letter saying that I could leave on a free. Cardiff wanted me – I went down and fancied it – all looked good and then the Club said they wanted a fee for me-, I couldn't believe it. To add insult to injury, I then broke my collarbone on the first day of training – game over then.

I then went to Leeds and trained there. Again, they wanted me. I was down to play for the first team v Ipswich. United held my registration still and guess what? Yup, they wanted a fee, it was a mess.

It really ended me as a footballer, although I had a good spell at Rochdale and won their player of the year award. It all boiled down to personality in the end. I still love SUFC and it is still the first result that I look for on a Saturday and think highly of the fans and many of the staff from that time. Football can definitely be a funny game.

FOOTNOTE

Steve is running a pub in the Midlands, around Brownhills, as far as I know. He phoned me a while ago to extend a welcome for official Blades coaches travelling to any games down there to stop in and see him – always worth knowing. He is happy to talk about his time in the game and, in particular, Sheffield United, and that makes him the ultimate mine host for a thirsty fan en route to a game.

He was custodian for the Club in one of our darkest hours. For my generation, as fans I cannot remember a bleaker feeling than the game against Walsall, although there are doubtless many younger fans who would argue that the wilderness years before Chris Wilder were as bad. I would argue that a drop into Division Four was nearly the end of the world, but it served to galvanize a generation, and the season that followed is one of the greatest in my time following the Club.

It is startling to see how Steve paid for standing up against the manager, a fact made harder because he had also paid £100,000, a fortune then, for the signature of Keith Waugh. Still honest, I remember this being one of the most straight interviews we ever did for the programme, and it makes fascinating reading even now.

GLEN COCKERILL

PLENTY TO CROW ABOUT

Glen is a player who, despite having a relatively short career as a Blade, is still held in high esteem by those who saw him play. I caught up with him as he made the car journey from home down to St Mary's to watch Saints play Manchester United a couple of years ago – on hands free of course!

I was born in Grimsby, but my family have strong Sheffield connections. Both Mum and Dad were from there – Dad came from High Green and all bar my maternal granddad supported Wednesday. He was a massive Blade and when I signed for the Club he was delighted!

Dad was a professional player and so was my brother. He started out with Huddersfield before joining Grimsby Town. He had over 10 years at Blundell Park and is regarded as a bit of legend by the Grimsby faithful. My brother John is also held in high esteem there.

I broke my leg as a youngster and that is probably how I came to miss the boat at Grimsby, so to speak. I was out for a while and it was a really bad injury. I was so desperate to play that when I was capable again I played in the net! As a player, I went and turned out for Louth Town in what was then the North Midland League from being just 16 – that toughened me up and I learned a lot.

We played Lincoln City in a tournament and I did really well. At that time, I was also working in an aerosol factory on Grimsby Docks – the manager at Lincoln then was Graham Taylor and he was a friend of my Dad's from his playing days with the Mariners, so we had good connections. I had a six-week trial and, as a result, Graham offered me a two-year deal. I never really looked back.

There were other figures there who would also have a part to play at Bramall Lane. Reg Brearley was on the board of directors and club secretary was Dick Chester. That was 1976 and the next couple of years there were very happy ones, and eventually I wanted to try something else – better myself if possible. Forest were keen, but Brian Clough wanted to have a better look at me. I was

impatient and Swindon Town, who then were having a go at it, offered me a great deal. Watford were keen. Graham was then the manager there along with ex-Imps Captain Sam Ellis, but they had been back to Lincoln for a few players and I was maybe one too many.

It didn't work out at Swindon for me to be honest. It was just one of those things – they had paid £120,000 for me and I didn't settle. I was abroad on holiday and I bumped into Lincoln boss Colin Murphy – he had sold me but was clearly keen to have me back – £40,000 was enough and back I went.

Like I said, when I joined the Blades a few seasons later it was right – the family connection made it an easy move for me and the fee was the same as Swindon had paid! I liked it straight away. There were some cracking lads in Keith Edwards, Colin Morris and Paul Stancliffe – the way I played suited Keith and 'Mozzer' and I think I refreshed them a bit with the way I played as well. I came, and there were still 10 games left to go. That was the season we went up, with Hull having to win by three clear points at Burnley. I watched Ceefax at home – they failed, and we went up. Promotion by Ceefax!

I settled in well and we bought a house two doors away from Colin Morris in South Anston – that was pretty useful as I managed to collect a driving ban! We used to drive through Rotherham and pick big Stan up on the roundabout in the middle where the nightclub was. If I said I took to Sheffield United, then I am pretty confident in saying that the fans seemed to take to me. I don't actually recall having too many bad games during my time there. I won quite a few of the different player of the year awards in my first season – the official and a fair few of the branches, and that meant a hell of a lot to me with the competition that I was up against.

To be honest, I think that it all began to unravel when Porterfield began to bring in the older and more experienced players in Like Peter Withe, Phil Thompson, Ken McNaught and the likes. Suddenly there were players really questioning what the Manager's decision was and it was new to Ian. Keith was always fairly outspoken but in a reasonable way. Some of the new players would knock on the door and voice their opinions. Phil was a top bloke. I really got on with him and respected what he had achieved in his career though.

I thought we had enough quality without going down that route. It was a decent side and, like I say, I had clicked with Keith and Colin. Southampton, who were a top-flight side, came in for me, and United felt it was the right thing to do in selling me to them. On this occasion I have to say that, for me, it was the right move to make. I embarked on a nine-year career at the Dell and loved my time there. Again, I picked their player of the year up in my first or second season, and that was a big achievement as the Saints ranks were packed with great players.

My boot boy was a lad called Chris Wilder. I know he was and still is a massive Blade – of course, he left the Dell and went back home. It is really good to see him doing well as a manager in his own right – he is a smashing lad and he didn't do a bad job with my boots back then!

I had spells with Orient and Fulham to name two and have also managed in the Non-League with Woking and came across Nigel, Gary Crosby, Andy Garner and Matt Brown when they were in charge at Burton Albion – what a top set of people they are, genuinely good lads who all know their football and will do the right thing for the Blades, of that I am sure.

I tend to watch Southampton when I can, and I still live just off the M25. Since leaving Woking I have changed my life dramatically – the Woking chairman encouraged me to do something different and, as a result, I learned the trade of tiling, and it has to be said that I really enjoy it. I have young children, so it means that I can pick when I want to work and spend plenty of time with them, and that works really well for me.

My Mum is still in Grimsby. Sadly Dad passed away in 2010 – I often think how lucky I have been down the years and how things have changed since I worked as a youngster in the Beachcomber Club at Humberston all of those years ago. I get back there a couple of times a year to see Mum and always come near to Sheffield on the way. I still keep in touch with a few of the lads and next year I will time my journey so I can come and see a game at the Lane. I always enjoyed my time there and they will always hold a special place for me.

FOOTNOTE

I loved Glenn Cockerill when he played for us. As he said, sometimes a player just clicks with the crowd from the off, and he was class for us in his time at the Lane. Before interviewing him I never knew that the Sheffield connection was so strong in the family. I knew there was a big link to Grimsby Town. The Mariners have always been a second club for me as most of the family settled over there before the war. If you were over there and they were at home, you would be dragged along to the game, it was as simple as that, and the Cockerill name there is highly regarded

I suppose that's the purpose of such interviews – to hopefully find out a few new things you didn't already know He was one of the few players of that era that I hadn't actually met since working here, and I wasn't disappointed. Also fascinating was the fact that Chris Wilder had been his boot boy at Southampton. At that time Nigel Clough was gaffer here, yet Glenn still made a big point of mentioning how big a Blade Chris is and how well he was doing in the League as a manager – maybe it was fate all along!

The offer is open to Glenn anytime he is travelling to see family and passing Sheffield to join us at a game as our guests. I bet there are a lot of fans that would make a hell of a fuss of him if he did.

GEORGES SANTOS

THE FRENCH CONNECTION

One of Sheffield United's more interesting characters of recent years is possibly Georges Santos – the second French player to sign for us after Lauren D'Jaffo. He is still a regular visitor to Bramall Lane well over a decade after his departure. Georges takes up the story of his time as a player and tells of his affections for the Blades and the Steel City, and the part he played in changing the history of English Football forever in the aftermath of the events known as the Battle of Bramall Lane...

I was born in Marseilles, which was an interesting place to grow up, and I came from a big family. I was always into football and learned my trade playing in the streets of where I grew up as a kid. I had been playing for Toulon when the chance to come to England materialised and I went to Tranmere Rovers on loan under the management of John Aldridge. I would play in the same team as quite a few future Blades in the shape of David Kelly and Andy Parkinson. The English game definitely suited my game.

My first encounter with Sheffield United came on a bank holiday at Prenton Park. It was a bit heated and the referee sent me off for punching Shaun Derry. I would not have minded, but it wasn't me. David Kelly admitted it was him after the game – not guilty!

I became a Blade from West Brom – Gary Megson had signed me from Tranmere for £25,000 to help fight relegation for the last eight games. I played my part and we stayed up. There was some doubt over a contract extension – I wanted two years and it wasn't to be – Neil Warnock stepped in and the rest is history.

I signed for Sheffield United on the same day as Keith Curle; in fact, it was Johnny Garrett who took me for my medical. My English wasn't too good then, but it was better than his French!

I was one of three French-born players at that time, so it was easy for me to fit in. I knew from the very first game that I would feel at home. Marseilles is a warm, passionate and very partisan place. Bramall Lane and its crowd mirrored it perfectly. I knew Laurent d'Jaffo as I had played against him in France when he was at Red Star and also in this country when I was with Tranmere and he was at Bury. We had exchanged phone numbers back then and we are still great friends today.

Patrick Suffo had trials with United before I joined when he was at Nantes – I though he had the potential to be a great player, if a little hot headed at times. We had a fantastic dressing room full of big characters. At that time I remember thinking just how many experienced pros there were – not a bad thing when you are scrapping to get every point, but it was funny how that would change in the course of a year.

Lee Sandford and Shaun Murphy were both natural leaders on and off on the pitch and Rob Page was a great Captain. Wayne Quinn and Curtis Woodhouse were youngsters getting a regular game and we were lucky that at that time we also had 'Jags', 'Monty' and 'Tongy' chomping at the bit to get a chance, so there were strong young players on the horizon.

Neil Warnock was always great with players. He knew when to scream and shout and also when a lad needed an arm around him. It was an art that helped get the very best out of what he had available.

In the 2000/01 season we had played against Forest at home. Famously in that game Andy Johnson elbowed me in the face, it was such a severe injury that my eye socket was smashed. My father was in the ground and he had to be called to the tunnel. The damage was so bad that the eye was hanging out at one point – a career-threatening injury.

I was in surgery for six hours and out of the game for four months. I have no problems with that – it is a man's game and such things happen. What I had the issue with was that at no point did Forest or the player check to see if it was OK or apologize in any shape or form – a shake of a hand would have been sufficient, but I heard nothing.

Fate dictated that the following year the player had joined West Brom, and we met them at Bramall Lane on March 19th, 2002. I was one of the subs –

things started badly and Simon Tracey was sent off fairly early on in the game. It was, to be fair, a bad-tempered match anyway, and there was no love lost between the two managers.

Myself and Patrick were put on as subs – warming up I felt and thought nothing – all I wanted to do was get on and do a job for my Club and its fans. The manager just told me to go out and play my game.

The tackle was, in all fairness, a little high. I had decided that the first one would let him know I was there and not prepared to be put upon again – it was a hard and full-blooded challenge, but the referee gave me a straight red and off I went. I remember being sat in the dressing room reflecting on what had happened as events unfolded on the TV. Within seconds Patrick was sat with me – he had head-butted their Captain in the fracas.

That was the last game I played for the Blades, as I believe was Patrick's. I always feel that I was made a scapegoat by certain people – the game was, of course, abandoned by the ref as we had insufficient players left to compete in line with FA rules – a first ever in the game due to sendings off and injuries. It was a heated moment and the whole incident was pinned on me and my actions.

I went to Grimsby Town and then to QPR and Brighton, amongst others; that said, I have always maintained my ties to Sheffield. My partner lives here and we have been together for a long time, so this is where I still live, and I love Sheffield and the people.

By the same token, I have always kept strong ties with Sheffield United FC. I am good friends with many of the staff, all who have been part of the family since I was a player, as well as many of the lads that I shared the dressing room with. The club is special to me – it is my team and I count myself very much as being a fan. I watch games whenever I can and still feel a part of it, although the manner of my departure makes me feel that I will always have unfinished business out on the pitch in a red and white shirt.

I think that I must be the only Cape Verdi International Footballer to ever live in Sheffield! That's where my parents hailed from and I made one appearance – I am a professional in all I do and I couldn't believe how badly it was all run back then – the players even had to pay their own air fares!

I am still involved in the game and I still love it. As I say, although born in Marseilles, Sheffield is my home and the Blades are my Club.

FOOTNOTE

I doubt there are many former Cape Verdi International Footballers who made their home in Arbourthorne! Georges is the original gentle giant – a million miles away from the image and reputation that he collected as a footballer in this country – a real gentleman.

It's hard to imagine that the events that day changed football history. By default, we became the first club ever to have a League game abandoned due to having an insufficient number of players left on the pitch to complete the game.

Georges has always maintained that, although high, the tackle was unintentional and without direct malice against the player. There is no doubting that there would have been an edge – the player had been involved in an incident that could have conceivably ended Georges career the previous season, leaving an eye socket so badly damaged that the eye itself was literally hanging out – terrible, although again without intention.

Despite the number of teams he played for after, the big man from Marseilles made Sheffield his home, and is a familiar figure around the city and Bramall Lane. He has worked as scout and agent for several clubs, so it is a fairly common site to see him at Blades' home games – it's like he never left to be honest!

He is an intelligent man who knows his football and speaks with eloquence – always engaging company and delighted to spend time with any Blade who shakes his hand and wants to share a few tales.

CHRIS MORGAN

CAPTAIN FANTASTIC

It has to be said, a certain kind of player fits with a certain kind of Club. Sheffield United fans have always taken to the no-nonsense characters who don't hide when they are having a bad game, give 110 per cent for the shirt and give the fans something to shout about. Chris Morgan had all of these qualities and more, which probably explains the reasons why he is still held in legendary status by the Lane faithful years after hanging up his boots as a player. Chris was an easy interview as he is still close to his SUFC colleagues. Let 'Morgs' tell his tale...

I grew up in Penistone near Barnsley and was obsessed by football from an early age. As a nipper I played for Hoyland Common Falcons as a striker of some repute – I kid you not!

There wasn't really any one Club that the family followed, but I was friends with the son of then Sheffield United Assistant Manager John McSeveney who worked with Ian Porterfield – that meant I got invited to plenty of Sheffield United games. It also meant that, after the match, we got upstairs in the South Stand to the old boardroom and directors' guests suite. There were always big bowls of sweets in there – ruffles I think, and I was well known for stuffing my face with them. If I went missing Dad knew where I would be – loading up my pockets!

I suppose that made an impression to me even then – United were a friendly, family club and we were always made welcome – it's still the case to this day.

I was scouted by Barnsley, and it was, I suppose, inevitable that I would join them as a schoolboy, although there were several other clubs having a look at me, but the Reds were the right choice for many reasons. It was OK signing for, say, Manchester United. They picked a lot of kids up from our area, but the chances of making it all the way through to the first team were slim. Dad always thought I had it in me to get through at Barnsley and gave me loads of encouragement when my head was down – he has always been a huge support as has all of the family.

IN OTHER WORDS

I made my Barnsley debut in a Premier League game away at West Ham on January 10th 1998. It was a bit of a torrid – we lost 6-0! That said, I got the man of the match, so I suppose that I did alright – it was a baptism of fire, but what doesn't kill you makes you stronger as a person, and I was always more than willing to learn.

The Manager who gave me my bow was Danny Wilson, and he is one of the very best that I have had the pleasure of working with – a true gent who knows how to get the very best out of players. He would also feature further on in my career as well – he has always been a big influence and friend to me.

My first taste of being sent off in the professional game was against Liverpool in March of that year. I was one of three reds players to be given their marching orders, mine for an incident with Michael Owen. I believe that I hold the record for red cards with both Barnsley and the Blades. Still not really sure what I think about that. I know I was a hard competitor – it's in my nature, but I never set out to be the pantomime villain once. I shudder to think how I would fair with the game and how it is today – I really do.

I cemented my place in the side under Dave Bassett – another great Manager. Looking back, I played in what could be argued were some of the best sides Barnsley has had in the modern era, and I am really proud of that.

'Harry' got us to the Play-off Final v Ipswich Town, which we lost. I got some stick for sitting on the pitch, head in hands with my back to the Tractor Boys' players as they went up the steps to collect their Winner's Medals and the trophy – papers said that I should have been stood there applauding them, but that wasn't what I felt like doing. I was devastated for the Club and fans, but also for the fact that I had missed the chance to get back to the Premier League as a player – Simple as that. I remember Steve Chettle picking me up and telling me not to worry as I would have other chances and days in big games that would end better than this – I took a lot from that as Steve had a great career and knew what he was talking about.

When I joined United it was at a time of trauma for Barnsley. The Club was in meltdown and the players had not been paid for several months. In fact, I had been at Cardiff for the Play-off Final v Wolves as a fan – a Blades-supporting mate had a spare ticket and we went down for the day – I knew Neil was interested – he had a stab at signing me the season before, but the fee asked was too high at the time, and I was gutted when it all went wrong v Wolves.

As I hadn't been paid for three months it meant I could sign for whoever I wanted – to be honest I was on my way to sign for Cardiff City – it had all but been agreed. The day before I was due to drive to Wales I went for a round of golf, and had my phone switched off. When I got back to the Club House I had a load of missed calls from my wife Natasha – I called her straight back thinking the worst, only to be told that Neil Warnock had been on the phone to her all morning and that I was signing for the Blades and not the Bluebirds – it was news to me!

Neil had got at my missus – sold the Club and what he wanted me to do in one phone call. Also, she didn't fancy moving to Cardiff, so blame my wife for landing me!

The team were in Cornwall, so I met Terry Robinson to discuss terms at Bramall Lane – I wanted to sign so it was easy. The first staff member I met when walking down the stairs from his office was John Garrett – he took one look at me, groaned and asked if what we had come to was signing a Barnsley donkey! Cheeky sod!

In fairness, it was an introduction to the banter and climate of the Lane, and a good one. The staff and togetherness there were, and still are, second to none. JG also became and remains a close friend of the family, as do many of the United staff, so I don't hold a grudge!

My first game was a friendly – tours under Neil were great. Some kid would turn up in the dressing room that you didn't know and get 30 minutes for the first team because he had decorated Neil's house – priceless!

He told me I would be playing in my position as usual – left wing. I looked at him dumbstruck, explaining I was a centre half – Neil responded by saying I was a left winger and that's where he had signed me to play – this carried on till I saw him wink at Kevin Blackwell – cleaver stuff – his way of easing me in and making sure there was no ego allowed. I think he did actually play me there for a bit as well!

There were some great lads – a strong dressing room and that's how Neil built and liked them. Rob Page, 'Kozzy', 'Browny', 'Jags', 'Monty' and 'Tongy' to name but a few. The first season wasn't great – a bit of a hangover from the triple assault to be honest. We also lost Michael Brown to Spurs and eventually Rob Page, who joined Cardiff City – 'Jags', although he protests to this day that he is a midfielder, was ready to step in to central defence – his natural pace and athleticism worked well with my more aggressive style – again, Neil had seen this and planned for the change.

I was made skipper – a proud moment for me. There was also a real air around the place that, for 2005/06 season, we were going to have a real go at it. In the summer Neil called me up to tell me he was thinking of signing Neil Shipperley – a lad I knew well from Barnsley. He had been brilliant at Oakwell, but to me had never really settled up north – the original chirpy cockney, 'Ships' always needed a phrase book to translate from South Yorkshire! I told him that, if he could get him, he would be a masterstroke both on the pitch and in dressing room.

I had spoken with him. He was at Palace under Ian Dowie, a manager who really worked on fitness and preparation – he was the fittest and lightest he had ever been, but miserable and not having a great time on the pitch. He told me he needed to put some weight back on!

Neil persuaded him that he could sign, stay in London Monday Tuesday, train Wednesday Thursday Friday, then play on a Saturday, heading straight home after the game. This meant he didn't have to uproot his family again. To me, in a team of warriors that season, 'Shipps' was one of the key players in getting the Club back up – superb.

I will never forget any of that season, but Danny Webber's goal v Cardiff that Bank Holiday Monday was special – we were almost there – only the Leeds result stood in our way. The lads got together and watched their game on Sky at the training ground and went wild when its conclusion saw us up. Never out of the top two all season, I think we became to first promoted runners-up to receive a medal for our efforts, and I treasure it.

Intent to give a penalty in the first game against Liverpool – never heard of before or again! That really played a big part in losing our place in the Premier League along with a few other strange decisions over the course of the campaign. Rob Hulse breaking his leg at Stamford Bride was also a big blow as he had been on fire for us. There was also an irony that a decisive penalty in the last game v Wigan would be taken by another player who had such a pivotal part in promotion in the form of Dave Unsworth after he was given a free by us.

When Neil departed he was replaced by Bryan Robson – a hero of mine. A top man, but not the right person for Bramall Lane at that point – the right man to take the Club back up was Neil – it was his team and we had learned we would have been stronger. That said, the players he brought in were brilliant – Beattie, Naysmith and many others. Kevin Blackwell was a good choice. He knew many of the lads and was a truly great coach, so we cracked on to the Play-off Final against Burnley.

I never saw us losing the Final – that's not me being big time, I just genuinely thought that we were more than good enough to take the step at Wembley – I still look back to this day and can't think why we just didn't turn up. I really can't, a huge chance lost.

My playing career was finished by an innocuous incident v Coventry down in the corner of the Kop and John Street – a nothing of a moment in terms of how I played the game. I carried on but knew something was wrong.

I saw a specialist the following day and he told me that it wasn't good news – the damage was severe and there was a good chance I would never play again. I wasn't prepared to just sit and take it – I did everything for two years to get back and play – I just had to admit that, in the end, it wasn't to be.

I was working up at Shirecliffe with the Under-21s and, in a small practice game, I decided to join in. One of the lads went around me, and as I turned to dive in with a challenge, I felt the knee go. I didn't make a fuss, I walked off the field, up to the changing rooms, took my kit off, picked up my boots and went upstairs to Danny Wilson's office. I threw open the door and threw my boots in the corner, the emotion and realization that I would never again pull on my beloved red and white stripes now made crystal clear.

Danny sat with his feet on his desk, regarding me with a wry smile on his face: 'You know, it's time 'Morgs', don't you?' were his words. I had fought long and hard – I never give up, but he was right. I had finished as a footballer and had to accept it.

I had been helping with coaching whilst trying to rehabilitate – the man who had given me my first real break was now helping me again. He opened his arms and, along with Frank Barlow, helped me take my first steps into being a football coach.

A lot has passed since then – a couple of spells as caretaker-manager linked in with coaching at Bramall Lane changed with the arrival firstly of David Weir then Nigel Adkins – new managers generally bring their own staff, although I had a great relationship with Nigel Clough. He understood my bond with the Blades and its fans, culture and history and really tapped into that. I enjoyed working with him. Another top bloke.

Once again it was Danny who played a part – he took me to Chesterfield as coach, although it didn't work out. I then had a spell with 'Browny' and David Kelly at Port Vale – again, results saw us part company.

I am now working as an agent for the company who represented me for many years – different territory, but one that I have seized with both hands and am really enjoying. It has given me the chance to spend more time with my young family whilst still having something to offer to the game, and its brilliant – it really is.

Would I like to coach again? Who knows? I always wanted to be a manager, but things and life change. It is about now and the job in hand, and I will treat that in the same way as I played the game.

I will always be grateful to Barnsley and the people there, like Norman Rimmington, God bless him. I was lucky, but when anyone asks me my Club there is only one answer. I will always be in love with Sheffield United, Bramall Lane and its wonderful fans. I am truly proud to have pulled on those famous red and white stripes and to have been its Captain. Chris Wilder is a tremendous manager who will take the Club far – he is also a top bloke and I have the highest regard for him as a friend and also as the man leading my beloved club.

One of my daughters now plays football so, with the success the Club is now having and its entrance to the WPL, who knows, one day you could see the name Morgan on the back of a United shirt again if that happened; I would be a very proud man indeed!

FOOTNOTE

Any interview with 'Morgs' would always be one of the longest – he is such a huge part of the fabric of the last 15 years at Sheffield United – added to the fact that he has a genuine bond with the Blades that can never be broken. I would imagine that, at times, its hard for him to come here and not be involved in some way. He watches many of the home games but is deliberately very low key, acting in his current role as agent and spotter of potential clients. That said, he now watches games as a fan, and that must also mean a lot.

Players like 'Morgs' don't really exist now. Much has changed in the game during the short time since his career ended. He played every game with heart and soul – uncompromising and carved from the granite of the Pennine Way, but also with fairness and the attitude of a true professional. Younger players such as Phil Jagileka and Kyle Walker credit his influence. Kyle still refers to him as 'The Skipper', and for good reason. If the bullets were flying and you had to go over the top of the trenches into battle, every one of us would want 'Morgs' at our sides, wouldn't we?

ALAN HODGKINSON MBE

BETWEEN THE STICKS

'Legend' is a word often used far too easily, especially in the game of football. Alan Hodgkinson was a Legend of the Lane in every sense. One of the Club's greatest-ever keepers, he epitomised every quality that is needed to play for the Blades. Working as a coach in football until his mid-70s, he took pride that Sheffield United was 'his' club, and always made a point of making sure those in his company knew just that. He sadly passed away in December 2015, but this interview was one that took place sat on a hotel balcony whilst he was in Malta acting as a Blades Ambassador during the sponsorship and friendship deal that played such a part in them being our official shirt sponsor. – let Alan tell his story…

I grew up in a small mining village between Rotherham and Sheffield called Thurcroft, and I was always keen on sport as a lad. I had a job as a butcher's boy in the Co-Op, but I got my chance as a footballer playing in the Midland League for Worksop Town at Central Avenue. There wasn't a lot of money around, but I loved every minute of it. Huddersfield Town, a big Club at the time, showed some interest, but nothing came of it. The Manager who came calling for my services was Reg Freeman at Sheffield United, and that suited me just fine!

The Worksop Manager called me into his office and told me that a gentleman's agreement had been made that I could go and have a trial with United's reserves and, if this proved successful, I could sign on my 17th birthday. The fee had been agreed at £250 for my services, and he told me that the Club needed it. At the time, I didn't even own a suit – my smart dress was a shirt and tie with trousers and a jumper – as a sweetener, he told me that, if I put pen to paper with United, they would buy me a suit! All I can say is that all these years after signing for the Blades I still haven't got it. I must tell Worksop they owe me a suit!

I loved going in to train at Bramall Lane – it was a magical place, and, in fact, it still is. It was on one of the early training sessions, on a Wednesday evening I think, that I learned something that would become an important part of how I developed my game.

IN OTHER WORDS

At the side of the old Cricket Pavilion there used to be these huge rollers – the really old-style ones for the cricket wicket – they were massive. The frame of them was really intricate and, by that time, very rusty ornate old-style iron work. Waiting for the trainer, I casually threw the ball at one, and it bounced off at quite an angle, so I had to move quickly to catch it. In fact, every time that I threw the ball in this way it never came back at me in the same place twice.

It was a great way to sharpen reflexes, and it became a big part of what I did. I loved that side of the ground – the smell was something all of its own – a piece of Victorian Sheffield that still sat there. There used to be old cricket benches there that you sat on for matches – you could even rent a cushion, so it made it a bit comfier. When they pulled the place down they sold a lot of these things off, and I was lucky to buy one. It sits in my garden in the midlands – a little bit of home from home and a place that I love.

I played for the reserves against Bury when I was still 16, and I made my debut in the Football League when I was 18. I had to work really hard as the number one back then was Ted Burgin – he had played for England and won the Second Division League Championship with the Club and was a really good keeper – also a big help to me as I looked to find my feet. As with many of the other lads back then, I had to do my time in the Army for National Service. I was in the Royal Signals, but I feel that this actually helped me develop as a person, although it did make it difficult for my United career and the Club was very good to me, as was Reg Freeman and then Joe Mercer. In fact, I made the first of my England under-23 appearances sandwiched between this and managing to turn out for the third team.

I finally became a first-team regular in January 1956 and then made my full England debut in April 1957 against the Auld Enemy – Scotland – at Wembley. A packed house, and it was truly amazing as I walked out of the tunnel with the noise. I felt really confident and proud that I had got to this stage after what was really so few league appearances. The unthinkable happened when really early in the game, I ended up picking the ball out of the back of the net – every keeper's nightmare!

I recovered OK, got four other England Caps and was part of the 1962 World Cup squad. I was never on a losing England side and met some truly great players that became good friends, people like the great Duncan Edwards, what a player, and Bobby Charlton, Jimmy Armfield and many others – they were fantastic days.

One of my biggest rivals was also the keeper at our neighbours, Ron Springett. He was one hell of a player as well – the two Sheffield clubs had some cracking lads back then and no mistake. At Sheffield United, I played in what is considered to be one of its all-time greatest defences, and for very good reason. Graham Shaw was a class player – very cultured and a great passer of the ball. He was also a real athlete – super fit and lightning quick. Cec Coldwell had come into the game late – like Graham, he was from the Sheffield area and we had signed him from Norton Woodseats. A Club Captain who made up for not being the greatest player technically by having a heart as big as a bucket and a real never say die attitude – a real leader who never knew when he was beaten and one of those that you would want with you in the trenches if the bullets started flying.

Brian Richardson was as hard as nails and another local lad – you really didn't mess with 'Richo' and he took no prisoners in his position. Gerry Summers was another classy footballer – cool, calm and seldom, if ever, flustered, no ball was ever wasted – he would become a good friend and I would eventually be his Assistant Manager at Gillingham, but that was much later on.

finally, there was Joe Shaw. What a player he was. I watched him in so many games and I swear I never saw him have to run for a ball. His reading and anticipation of the game was remarkable. He just knew where to be and when. Nothing was ever booted down the pitch, every pass was considered, inch perfect and measured – to me, Joe invented the role of sweeper in the English game and didn't even know it. One of the very best I ever had the privilege of playing with.

I always had a real bond with the fans. I would run up to the Kop and they would sing my name – I didn't know how to respond. At the time the biggest programme on TV was called *Gunsmoke* – a Cowboy programme, so one day I decided to point my fingers at them and shoot like I had a pair of sixguns! They loved it and I kind of stuck – it was my trademark!

The FA Cup Semi-Final against Leicester was a moment lost for us. I really believe that the team we had at that point was more than capable of going on to lift the Cup – we were that good on our day – two replays after the first game saw us lose and Leeds United went onto the Final. I still look back and wonder what we could have achieved – I would have loved to have played for the Blades in an FA Cup Final. In my day, it was one of the highest accolades if you got to the Final – these days it seems so undervalued and it's a shame.

We were promoted that season, so it kind of evened itself out, but a double would have been good!

Life with United was always interesting, and we had some fantastic overseas tours under John Harris – working-class lads getting a chance to jet around the globe – incredible times for us all. In 1962 we went out to tour the USA and Canada for nearly a month and in 1965 we went out to Australia and New Zealand with Blackpool to play a series of games, contesting a trophy known as the BOAC Cup – we won it as well. Such travel was only in the dreams of most of our fans at that time.

Harris built another great side that went for promotion in the 1970/71 season. Lads who had been around a while with me, such as Alan Woodward and Gil Reece had players like Eddie Colquhoun and Tony Currie added to the ranks and we really went for it, playing some lovely stuff. It was the manager who decided that my career was over. We were playing away at Oxford United and, when we arrived at the hotel, John Hope was sat in reception. I found out that we had swapped John Tudor for he and David Ford to bolster the promotion push – fair enough, but nothing had been said to me about it.

I knew that I hadn't been brilliant in the last few games, but genuinely felt that, after all of my service and loyalty, I could have been treated much better. I had a run in with the board a year or so before when they said that money from my testimonial game had gone missing from the turnstiles and that had left a bad taste if I am honest. The manager took me on one side and finally told me that he would be playing John Hope in the game, and I wished the lad well. In fact, he was bloody good for the rest of the season and played a big part in sealing promotion.

The following year he seemed to lose all confidence and was letting a few howlers in – I was still very much a part of the coaching staff, even though I had vowed that, as a player, that was me done. The Manager came to me and asked me to play – I was still more than capable and knew it, but, call me bloody minded, but I told him he had decided that I was finished when he brought the lad in, and as far as I was concerned that was that.

When I left Bramall Lane, it was a hard decision, but I wanted to coach and had the chance to join my old friend and teammate from the Blades, Gerry Summers, at Gillingham. I liked it down there and enjoyed my time. We had some great players including a young Steve Bruce and also Micky Adams, who went on to have a good career – well, the pair of them did. When it came to an end there I hit on the idea of becoming what was the first-ever full-time professional goalkeeping coach.

We moved to Dunchurch in the Midlands as it was ideally placed to travel to wherever I was coaching. I was at Ibrox with Chris Woods and Rangers, Arsenal with David Seaman, all over the place, and I loved the life. I sat on both benches when Wednesday played Arsenal in the FA Cup Final – one each half as I did both of their keepers! I bet I am the only coach to do that – I never wore a Wednesday badge though, I promise!

Manchester United were another of my employers, and I became great friends with Sir Alex – he sent me out to look at a keeper for him to say what I thought. I reported that the lad was top class and he should sign him. Thankfully he listened and, as a result, I became the coach and mentor of Peter Schmeichel – in my opinion one of the very best that the game here has ever seen.

I also worked for the Scottish FA as well as running courses for the FA and all around the world – it was one of the best thigs I ever did.

I have ended up at Oxford United – not far from home and a Club which has a Manager who is going places – his name is Chris Wilder. Like me, he is a Blade through and through and, without a doubt, one of the best young coaches I have ever worked with – I am telling you, he has a really bright future in the game and he is driven and determined, but with a touch of the old school type of management about him.

He will manage at the highest level, of that I am sure. I hope that one day he gets a shot at Sheffield United, as I think he would be an amazing fit for the Club, I really do.

It was a great surprise and honor to be awarded the MBE for my services to the game and something of which I am very proud indeed – over 50 years is a long time in any industry and I am humbled that people deemed me worthy, I really am.

I never thought I would still be coaching at 74, but I relish every moment. It keeps me young and also out from under Brenda's feet! I had a major heart bypass a number of years ago. I have never smoked, keep fit and do everything in moderation, so it just goes to show how careful you have to be. Since then I have seized every day and any opportunities it can bring.

I love Bramall Lane and Sheffield United – every keeper I have trained that has played there gets the same warning – walk carefully in those steps towards the Kop because they are mine – it's as simple as that. I get back when I can, and it is always home. I didn't get chance to return for a while as I was so busy. When the day came, I walked up the tunnel to the end. It was raining, and the ground was still empty. As I walked out it brought back all the emotions and feelings along with all the great memories. Wonderful – my wife still says that I love the Blades more than her!

FOOTNOTE

Alan retired at the age of 76 and his next job was to write his superb book *Between the Sticks* – we held the launch at Bramall Lane and he and his family, along with many well wishers and former colleagues, filled the Platinum Suite as he did a Q and A about his life. 'Hodgy' had the strongest handshake that I have ever encountered – it could crush bricks, and I think that it was, in some ways, a bit of a test in case you winced! He was sussing you out – seeing what you were made of.

Of all the former players I have had the pleasure of dealing with, there were none better. A true legend and our second-highest appearance maker in the Club's history, he was, quite rightly, proud of his achievements in the game and proud of the fact he had represented the Blades for so long and with such distinction.

A strong man with old school values, you could soon sense the emotion in his voice when the subject of the Blades came up. Retirement saw him attend most home games, he and Brenda driving up to dine upstairs and enjoy things from the comfort of the boardroom, and he loved it.

Sadly, Alan fell into ill health, although we still kept in regular contact and I went down to see him at home, driving was difficult and then an impossibility. It seemed strange without him there on a match day.

He died in December 2015, and with his passing went out one of Bramall Lane's brightest lights. He was one of our favorite sons.

The first game after we lost him was against another club he had coached, Coventry City, live on Sky. He had passed away the night before much-loved Club Photographer Martin Harrison, and wreaths were laid in front of the Kop, 'Hodgy's' by George Long, the young United keeper who had come through the ranks and of whom the great man had high hopes for a top career.

As he walked up to the Shoreham end with the floral tribute, I asked him to shoot the fans in the same way as the great man once did, and he duly obliged – a nice touch in genuine tribute to the legend in whose footsteps he was indeed treading.

They don't make them like Alan any more – they really don't, and his wish to see Chris Wilder take charge of Sheffield United also came true – it's so sad that he wasn't still around to have enjoyed that moment – he would have loved it.

ANDY TAYLOR

TAYLOR MADE FOR THE JOB?

Andy had a bitter sweet time with the Blades after joining from Tranmere. I spoke with him a couple of seasons ago, ahead of his return with then club Walsall, as he reflected on what could have been for him in S2...

I started out with Blackburn Rovers at a time when they were always finishing in the top half of the Premier League and in European contention. As a result, the competition for a first-team place was pretty hot and I ended up banging on the door a few times to get out on loan. I got out to a few clubs including Blackpool, Crewe, Huddersfield and QPR. Ian Holloway was brilliant there – a real character and no mistake. I had three months in London but really didn't fancy living down there. I had a spell also at Tranmere Rovers that also proved successful, so much so that I made the move there a permanent one.

I had 18 months at Prenton Park, which was a good time for me – so much so that a few of the big boys came sniffing round – Coventry City was one, Forest another, but I met with Kevin Blackwell for talks and he brought me down to Bramall Lane for a look round. I can well remember walking out in to the stadium for the first time. What really hits home is the size of the Club – it really is huge in every way – instantly impressive. When you set out as a young footballer it is the sort of club that you aspire to play for. No disrespect to the others, but there was no real contest.

It was also a coincidence that I had the same agent as Chris Morgan. I always trusted his advice and he said that 'Morgs' was a good lad and would help me to get settled in – that made things choice-wise even easier to make – I signed and became a Blade. The team had already set off for a pre-season trip to Hungary, and I had to meet them at the airport to fly out.

They were easy to spot as all of the lads were well kitted out in their tracksuits. I was in jeans and a shirt as I had literally just put pen to paper

– I made my way over and through the crowd moved the shape of Chris Morgan. 'Morgs' had his angry face on – that scowl that is unique to Chris was well cemented on his face. Its only when you get to know him that you learn that's how he looks all the time – back then I didn't know whether he was going to take my hand and shake it or grab me by the throat and do the same. Luckily, he shook my hand, smiled and welcomed me to the Blades!

It was a great set of lads with some really big hitters around at that time – Gary Speed was brilliant and there were others like 'Monty' and 'Quinny' to name but a few. That was the really startling thing to be honest. The Club that I joined was chock full of real quality – a top Championship side that was going to be there or thereabouts in terms of challenging for a return to the Premier League. The United that I left three years later was stuck in Division One. Incredible – the Club really is huge and I still can't get my head around what happened.

My first season went pretty well – I made over 30 appearances and settled into Yorkshire life – like I said, who wouldn't relish playing for a Club like United. It was a fair step up from Tranmere and it took time to adjust, but I worked hard. When I got injured it was exactly the same that did for 'Morgs' – I ruptured my cruciate and lateral ligament on Boxing Day against Hull City. That was just about my luck to be honest – one hell of a late Christmas present and one that kept me out of the game for a long time.

There are some quality people behind the scenes at Sheffield United and they are as much a part of keeping you going when times are bleak as the physios, coaches and teammates. It was a long hard battle, but thankfully I won it and played again – 'Morgs' didn't, so I have to be thankful for that and I know it.

The team was, of course, relegated and Danny came in. That first season kind of summed up my time at the Club again – issues off the pitch conspired towards preventing automatic promotion and it all went down to the Play-off Final at Wembley v Huddersfield Town. I was on the bench and came on for virtually the last kick of the game. The gaffer turned around and asked me if I would take one of the imminent penalties. We had practiced them all week and I had been banging them in – of course I felt up for it.

I stepped up and felt comfortable – there was never a doubt in my mind. I thought I struck the ball cleanly and well – goal. That was until I saw the ball bouncing back towards me. I was gutted – all the things that went through my head in the aftermath I still recall today – the fans – we should have been back in the Championship and we had blown it. Others had missed before me, not that it made it any better. I knew there would be job losses – people who couldn't pay their mortgage as a result – the fall out was massive. I have never felt like that in my life. It was terrible.

In a sense taking the pen was a lose-lose situation, I suppose. If you score and win you are a hero, miss and cock up you are a zero – there are no in between parts to it – all or nothing, and when you think of the responsibility of it all it really is incredible. That again summed my time as a Blade up, and I often think of what would have been had we gone up – not so much from a contract perspective – my deal was over, but I suppose you wonder what would have been, would I have got another year? Who knows?

I joined Walsall eventually and am lucky – it is a great Club to play for and the Manager has been brilliant to me. I loved Sheffield United even though my time there was a tough one. I will always feel that the fans never really saw the best of me and, for that reason, I will always regard it as being unfinished in terms of business. I still have a lot of good friends there and wish the Club well – that is apart from when we have to play them!

FOOTNOTE

Andy Taylor was always a great lad to have around the place – a good character and hardworking, that bad injury against Hull City would be a blow to all, but he cracked on and did all he could to get back as quickly as he could – you never heard him moan or complain as he battled in the gym and with treatment as teammates were out on the training pitches.

The comments he makes about coming off the bench and being asked to take a penalty in the Play-off Final v Huddersfield are interesting, and kind of sum the lad up. For many players, the fact that they had missed a penalty in such a game would be enough, yet Andy's thoughts were for the staff behind the scenes who would struggle to keep their livings as a result of the failure to secure pro-motion.

At the time of writing he had been released by Blackpool following a couple of seasons there – a mate of mine who is a huge Tangerines fan rated him and said much the same about his attitude as most do. It's tough now when you are a professional footballer without a Club, there are many at this time of year out of work and wondering what their agent can do to get them fixed up. All I know is that, if a manager is after a decent little player with an attitude that will never let a Club down, he can look no further than Andy Taylor, and we wish him all the very best in getting sorted out somewhere.

ASHLEY FICKLING

NOTHING FICKLE ABOUT ASH

Ashley Fickling is a name that many of an age will remember as being there or thereabouts in the days of Dave Bassett. The defender wore the famous red and white shirt on just a few occasions, but the Sheffield lad went on to make a fair few League appearances elsewhere before injury ended his career. I spoke with him over the New Year a few seasons ago to find out where the game had taken our one-time hope from the ranks of the youth team…

I was a Birley School lad and loved my football. I know that some say it, but I was a mad Blade, as were all the family, so it was always United that mattered. Before I signed I was training firstly with Wednesday and latterly with Barnsley. Kevin Fogg, who would go on to make such a significant contribution in the early days at the Sheffield United Shirecliffe complex, was a big influence there, as was ex-Blade Frank Barlow, but when Dennis Finnegan came knocking on our door to see if I fancied United there was no contest.

I signed schoolboy forms and then, when the time came, Dave Bassett was the one who gave me the chance me as an apprentice pro, although it was technically Billy McEwan who made me a Blade, and I owed him a lot for that. I also played for England at schoolboy level as well as Under-18, so the decision to become a Blade was a good one.

Dane Whitehouse and Mitch Ward were just a couple of years older than me, and there was a strong Sheffield feeling in the dressing rooms as players like Chris Wilder, Jamie Hoyland, Carl Bradshaw and Brian Smith were all around to offer advice and support – it was just as well as we had a fair few cockney accents around at that time!

We had a massive squad and that meant that it was hard sometimes to get a shout in the first team, and I played plenty of reserve matches in the meantime. I got my chance on a Tuesday night on October 8th 1991 in a League Cup replay at Bramall Lane against Wigan Athletic in front of around 6,500 hardy souls, and I got the number-two shirt – I thought I did reasonably well and we progressed to the next round with a Jamie Hoyland goal. 'Harry' couldn't have agreed, however, because that was my last shout of the season!

I got a few run outs in the League Cup a while later and I was part of the squad taken out to Piacenza in the Anglo Italian Cup by Wally Downes. I played in the number five there in what was a 2-2 draw and that was a great experience. I had missed out on the home game at Bramall Lane against Udinese, which was a strange one to say the least. We had Nathan Blake, Glynn Hodges, Charlie Harfield and Dave Bassett sent off, accompanied by a player called Kozminski for the Italians. I also played in the 3-3 draw with Ancona and a 4-1 victory over Cesena away.

When I wasn't getting a chance, it was Billy McEwan who came to my rescue and took me up to Darlington on a three-month loan. I think that was the maximum time then. To be honest, I loved it. Billy was marmite to a lot of Blades, but for me and a few others he was brilliant, and I played virtually every game up there.

Returning to United meant coming home, but it also meant back to the reserves, and I didn't want that once I had the bit between my teeth. I had torn my metatarsal at Darlo and came back to Bramall Lane. I did my rehab under Derek French and Dennis Circuit – they were brilliant and thankfully I didn't need the operation – it healed by itself.

When I left the Lane, I joined Grimsby Town under Brian Laws – another Manager who would play a big part in my career. 'Harry' had offered me another year but I needed to get out. I was there when the now infamous incident happened between Brian and Italian football legend Ivano Bonetti. We had lost a game late on and the gaffer was fuming – as we got back in the dressing rooms, Bonetti helped himself to a chicken leg as if nothing was wrong. What happened and the expletives that followed are part of football folklore – a real clash of cultures!

I loved it there before I re-joined Brian when he became Manager of Scunthorpe United – again, I had three great years there before injuries once more got the better of me. A figure that loomed large with his advice at Glandford Park was the then physio Nigel Adkins. He was another top lad who tried to help me get playing again. He also asked me what I was going to do when I had to finish playing as a pro – I think he had a good idea that all was not well.

It was he who got me interested in the idea of becoming a physio myself – as I had paid into the PFA from being young I took advantage of one of the courses that they designed for people such as me – apart from a spell as a non-contract player at Scarborough (where I got injured again) I was done and took a four-year course that saw me qualify as a physiotherapist in my own right. Nigel took an interest and I really owe him for that. Of course, he has shown what a shrewd cookie he is and gone on to become a great manager, a great man-manager and no mistake.

I was done at 28, but the PFA offered me a route to stay in the game and I love it. I am the head physio at the Sheffield Wednesday Academy – I have been here since 2007 and I'm proud to be able to give something back to the game.

Attitudes and skills change – for instance, one of my clearest memories as a youngster at United were the pre-season army camps that Dave Bassett sent us on – they were bloody brutal, I can tell you! But that said, the team spirit was second to none, that's why I persevered for so long.

My family are all still very much season-ticket holders at Bramall Lane, and I get there when work allows. I am proud of my time there and the fact that it set me on the road to a career in the game.

FOOTNOTE

Ash made it out onto the park in the red and white stripes and realized a childhood dream. He also knew that, if he was going to have a chance as making it in the game, he probably needed to move on to get the chance. He is well regarded and remembered at both Grimsby Town and Scunthorpe United as a player, and quite right too – Ash was a good player and always gave his all for the cause.

It is also interesting how big a part former Blades manager Nigel Adkins has played in the path that he decided to take after injury ended his playing days as a pro. Everyone needs that bit of sound advice when the choice has to be made, I have lost count of the number of players who simply lose their way once that day-to-day routine of being a player is taken away for them.

It would be fair to say that Nigel didn't have the best of times at Bramall Lane during his tenure, and for a wide variety of reasons, but his journey from player to physio to promotion-winning manager at several clubs has been well noted, and Ash took the advice he was given.

At the time of writing, Ash is still with our neighbours and the Fickling family are still very much Blades!

TONY CURRIE

STILL DOING MAGIC

Because I see and speak to TC most days of the week, it's easy to forget that there is a generation of Blades and more who never saw him play professional football for Sheffield United yet have been weaned on the stories of his style, swagger and sheer quality in the red and white shirt. To say he is an iconic figure for the Club would be an understatement – he epitomises the Club that he loves so much and stands out as arguably one of the most talented players ever to ply his trade in the Steel City – TC talked to me about his journey and why he came home…

I was born and bred in North London and from an early age I was football mad. I lived in our house with my Mum, brother, grandparents, uncles, aunts and every family member you could imagine! It was a bit like a commune, but it gave me a huge and very warm family unit, if a bit unorthodox. Bert and Jim, my uncles, were a huge support. Bert, a Chelsea fan, used to take me to Stamford Bridge from being about eight, so Chelsea became my team and my hero was and still is Jimmy Greaves – one of the greatest goal scorers there has ever been. Jim was a Gunner's fan, and both used to travel up to Sheffield and to away games when I was a Blade – they were my biggest supporters – my local team was Hendon in the Isthmian League, and I also used to go and watch them when I could.

I played football as a kid at school and had trials for Chelsea and also for QPR that were unsuccessful – the latter being ironic that many years later they would have to pay £450,000 for my services when I left Leeds. I was also a decent cricketer and had the chance to also go on the ground staff for Surrey when I left school, but it was football that beckoned me – it was all I wanted to do.

When I left school, I got a job on a building site and played local league stuff – I was spotted by Watford and offered a trial with them. I did well and was, as a result, offered an apprenticeship at Vicarage Road. The manager was Ken Furphy who would play a part in my later career, again at the Blades.

I worked hard and got my first chance as a sub in a League Cup game at Stoke City in September 1967 as a 17-year-old. Three days later I made my home League debut against Bristol Rovers and scored two. In fact, in my first 17 full League appearances for the Hornets, I scored nine goals that included two hat-tricks, and I was also capped for England Youth level.

Top flight Clubs were watching me, and it was Sheffield United who swooped. A fee was agreed of £26,500 with an agreement that the sale was deferred until Watford were knocked out of the FA Cup. It was ironic that Sheffield United were the Club that did it! I came to Sheffield and signed for John Harris on February 1st – a big move for a lad just turned 18 from the South.

I scored on my League debut against my hero Jimmy Greaves and Spurs with a header at the Bramall Lane end on Monday February 26th and it began a love affair with the Club and fans that is still so strong today. I missed the next game away at Leicester, and here is one for the fact fiends – I has already made arrangements before the deal to get married to my first wife, so I missed the game to tie the knot! John Harris did all he could to persuade me that he could have a fast car in London to get me to Filbert Street straight after, but I didn't think she would be too happy with that!

It was a strange season as we got relegated, and with what I thought was a decent team. John Harris moved upstairs, and Arthur Rowley came in as Manager – a Football League scoring legend if ever there was one. Arthur made some good signings that went on to become Blades legends – Ted Hemsley and Eddie Colquhoun were two of them. He also brought John Tudor in, but things didn't quite gel and we ended the season in ninth, even though I had really begun to settle in the city and we had moved into our Club house at Meersbrook on Bishop Court Road – Joe Shaw had once lived there with his family, so it was very much a 'United' feeling there.

Arthur departed, and John Harris came back in – the gaffer was very good to me – he was very much an old school Man-Manager – he didn't swear, was a strict Methodist and a tee-totaller – he had been a hard-as-nails Captain for Chelsea and a good player in his day, but he knew how to get the best out of you. He never ranted or raved in the dressing rooms at half time – he left that side of the business to John Short and he could give it out, let me tell you.

IN OTHER WORDS

The team that won promotion in 1971 was one of, if not the, best that I had the privilege of playing in. every day in training at the Ball Inn was a joy – the friendships that were made all of those years ago are still as strong today. Sadly, a few of them have passed away, but those left all stay in touch and we get together when we can. Len, Ted, Frank Barlow, Billy Dearden, Eddie Colquhoun and Geoff Salmons are all still local – a great bunch of lads that I regard as brothers, not just mates.

I get asked when I do Q and A's who is the best player I ever played with. There is no contest at any level – it was Alan Woodward – one of the greatest wingers of his generation.

We just knew instinctively what the other was thinking on the pitch – he knew just where to be, and I knew exactly where to drop the ball from any angle. A phenomenal athlete with the hardest and most accurate shot there was – to watch him pick the ball up and attack a defense was magnificent – he should have had a bag full of England Caps. Alf Ramsay famously didn't play with wingers, but the way 'Woody' played meant that he could just cut in to the centre forward position seamlessly as someone else dropped back in to cover. We were so fluid as a side in the way we played. He also never really had the self confidence you would expect. Half time always saw the toilet door closed and a plume of fag smoke appearing from above. I loved him to bits – I often think that England should have played us together in the International side – we would have been brilliant together for our country.

That campaign was special – the last home game, again, against my old team Watford is ingrained in my mind forever. When I see that picture of us all in the dressing rooms after with the champagne I just think 'now that's a team' – very special people, very special memories.

I loved the Club and still do. The following season that saw us top the table at one bit was great. We played a certain brand of football and we wanted to entertain the fans, and I think they appreciated that. I juggled two lives as my first wife wasn't well at times – I had to go home from training and deal with young children and keeping the family going as well as being a professional football player. I think that also people expect me to be the character that I was on the pitch – flamboyant and self-confident, and that can be easy when you are, in a sense, an actor on a stage. The real me is quiet and, at times, a bit shy of the attention – that's all.

I could have joined Manchester United as the replacement for Bobby Charlton when he retired, but I opted to stay at the Club I loved, and signed a rolling contract in 1973 that effectively tied me to Sheffield United for the best years of my career – something I was happy to do as I had been assured by the Chairman that we would keep our best players and invest to build a team round me – that was music to my ears as this was home. The promise became a tad hollow when, at the end of the season, another big friend and outstanding talent in Geoff Salmons was sold to Stoke City in the following closed season – it was crazy. Why sell your best players when we had a chance of achieving something?

1974/75 saw me proved wrong to an extent – my old manager from Watford, Ken Furphy, had joined the Blades the previous December and we missed the League Championship title by four points and also narrowly missed out on a place in Europe – so tight were things at the top. Again, we could and should have kicked on. Sad to think that it still remains the Club's highest League finish since.

My last season was a nightmare. We just couldn't buy a win and were as good as relegated by Christmas. Furphy was sacked in October – Jimmy Sirrell, who had done wonders on a shoestring for Notts County, was his replacement. He was a good football man, but a little strange in his approach. We had some really good youth coming through around that time – Tony Kenworthy, Keith Edwards, Simon Stainrod and a few others were really promising, as their careers would show, but he seemed reluctant until it was too late. I think Ted Hemsley, who tended to be a voice from the dressing rooms, told him early on that if he didn't play them then we would go down. He was right.

I had no choice – I had an England career and that would not be furthered in the old Division Two. The club also needed the money, so I joined Leeds United – one of the Clubs we always regarded as a real rival. They were still one of the biggest clubs in the country, even though, like at Bramall Lane, many of their greats were reaching career ends and they were beginning to re-build and go again.

I enjoyed Leeds and played some of my best football there. That meant several Semi-Finals, but I never managed to get that Cup-Winner's Medal there that a good side came close to touching a few times. I got the goal of the season for them as well for my effort against Southampton.

I also got a few more England Caps there, but it was always going to be hard when Don Revie was manager. Alf Ramsay had made me Captain of the Under-23s and he had the same role in mind for me for the full team, but, of course, was sacked after we failed to qualify for the World Cup in 1973. Early in his career, Revie had the 'mavericks' together – players like me, Frank Worthington, Stan Bowles and Alan Hudson together to basically say that we weren't his type and that we probably wouldn't be involved as much – although I made most of the squads the actual appearances proved that he was, if anything, a man of his word! I think I was better than the 17 Caps that I won, but I am grateful for each and every one of them, as well as being intently proud – of that you can be sure.

From Leeds I went to QPR and Captained them in the FA Cup Final replay v Spurs – some may remember that I gave away the bloody penalty that cost us the cup – it was my life ambition to win it and I vividly remember walking up the steps to receive my runner's-up gong and looking at the famous old trophy, wishing that it was my turn to pick it up for the Club and for myself. It wasn't to be, but the medal is one of my prized possessions.

I was signed for QPR by Tommy Docherty – I was injured at the time and didn't kick a ball in anger for the Hoops for what seemed like an age, and the fans must have wondered what they had got. My wife had wanted to move back nearer to family in London, otherwise I would have remained settled at Leeds. Arsenal wanted me, but Leeds didn't really want me to join a Club that were rivals in the same division. QPR were in the old League Two and matched the £450,000 bid, although I think that Anderlecht also had a nibble. 'The Doc' was replaced by the best coach I ever worked under – Terry Venables – years ahead of his time, he was one of the game's greatest innovators. I think he should still be England manager to this day. He was brilliant for me even though injuries were really beginning to take their toll, along with the plastic pitch at Loftus Road.

When I left QPR I attempted to play for Southend, but again got a bad knock. With my professional career as good as over, I had also gone to Canada for a spell, but was never paid and messed around – I had all on raising the money to get myself back – it was disastrous and, coupled with the end of my first marriage, they were bad times – very bleak. I drove a taxi for a spell and also took a job doing soccer schools over the summer for Haven Leisure. I had a Fiat Panda, a bag with a few balls and a few cones in, and that was it. I recall setting one up at their place in Hayle and only one kid turning up with his Dad, who happened to be a Blade and a big fan.

My testimonial, given by Sheffield United, was a huge turning point in my life. It gave me a huge piece of self-respect back as well as some stability – things I will always be grateful of. The game itself, on the back of a year of events, was the biggest at the Lane that season – even though my knee was in bits, I managed to play a part and that was as a thank you for the wonderful fans that were there for me as ever.

A short time later, I became Head of the Football in the Community Project and worked around the schools of the City and surrounding areas taking football to them. I also ran the birthday parties and half-term soccer schools and camps. I loved every minute of it and still bump into fully grown adults that I coached when they were knee-high to me – magical stuff.

For the last decade I have been the Club Ambassador – that involves representing United at a whole host of events. I also get involved with ground tours and hospital visits, so I am still as busy as I have ever been.

I love Sheffield United FC. They are my Club, and I have a kinship and bond with the Blades and its fans that is really something very special indeed, especially after all of these years. 2018 will mark 50 incredible years since I put pen to paper on that February day in 1968, and I wonder where it has all gone. The time has just flown. I have spent 40 years of my life as a part of this Club, and the Club and fans are a part of me.

Although I have never lost my southern accent, I am a proud Sheffielder and Blade who is grateful for the chance it gave me and love the fans have showed me to this day.

FOOTNOTE

Voted the greatest player in our history at the Club 125 event in 2014, it is always interesting to see the life and memories that one of our greatest sons has of Sheffield United and his life in general. I have worked closely with him for over two decades and would like to think that I know and understand him as well as anyone.

He is a quiet, unassuming man who, when you get to know him, is devastatingly funny and mischievous to the last. I recall walking through the old sponsors lounge upstairs one evening as the legend attempted to clean up the mess of yet another birthday party as the kids ran riot and the parents present stood round and chatted. As he shoveled used paper plates into a black bin liner, he looked at me and uttered the immortal words, 'I used to play for England, you know!' I have told him many times that this should be the title of any autobiography on him!

He loves the Club, and it would be fair to say that the Club loves him still. A 'This is Your Life' event at Bramall Lane to celebrate those 50 years sold out within minutes – a measure of the legacy of his association with Sheffield United FC. Tony was made a Non- Executive Director of Sheffield United FC in 2018, shortly after seeing the South Stand renamed the 'Tony Currie Stand' – yet further marks of appreciation for the man voted the Blades greatest ever player.

CARL BRADSHAW

BOTH SIDES OF THE CITY

There are still a relative few who have played for both Sheffield Clubs with success – the Warnock years saw the signing of what, at the time, were three of their best players – Quinn and Bromby directly followed by Derek Geary by way of a spell at Stockport County. Not many are Sheffield born and bred and known out and out for supporting the opposition. Carl Bradshaw is one of the few – as Sheffield as a bottle of Hendo's, he tells the story of his journey from red to blue to red and beyond, with a few hiccups along the way!

I was born in Sheffield and went to City School. It was great there – a lot of different characters as it sat in the middle of the Woodthorpe, Hackenthorpe and Woodhouse areas of the city – you had to learn to stand up for yourself and it was a good grounding for later life.

I always played football for the school and also Sheffield Boys – I also turned out for Woodhouse Angel so I was busy most of the time! My elder brother Darren was also a very good player, and it added to a competitive atmosphere that pushed me a little bit harder to succeed. He had played in the Sheffield Schools side that won the Gillette Cup by beating Coventry over two legs – the Final being at Bramall Lane. I was in the side that matched that feat two years later when my year beat Swindon – I don't think there are many brothers who have both achieved that in the city.

I joined Sheffield Wednesday as an apprentice. Mates asked me how I could do that when I was a Blade, but it was an easy choice. They were a big Club with fantastic facilities – some may disagree, but I think that back then they had the edge over Sheffield United as far as it went. I enjoyed all of my time there, and I mean that. As much as United mean to me, they gave me a chance and top-quality coaching as well – they made the youngsters feel like pros.

One man who made a big impression with me and had a lot to do with our sessions was John Harris. The man who is a legend in Blades terms had

joined Wednesday under Jack Charlton after being shown the door at United – some reward for all he had done for the Club over the years, but that's football.

I listened to all that he said. Here was a man who had played and managed at the very highest level. He had looked after names like Joe Shaw, Tony Currie and Alan Woodward, and it was a pleasure for me to be in that sort of company. Brilliant.

I signed professional forms but made my Football League debut when I was sent out on loan to Barnsley where Alan Clarke was manager. They had a tidy little side there – David Hirst was beginning to make a name and they also had Steve Agnew and former Owls defender Mark Smith in their ranks. I really enjoyed the chance.

I scored on my League debut against Crystal Palace on August 23rd 1986, and the ball hit the back of the net after 38 seconds. I reckon that must be one of the fastest debut goals ever! The experience did me good as when I went back to my own Club after the loan spell I netted for Wednesday on my debut for them as well!

Like I say, I loved my time at Hillsborough – I was doing what I had always dreamed of doing for a big Club, and I must confess that even I was surprised when the chance to join Manchester City came along – Wednesday wanted to bring Imre Varadi back and I was wanted as part of the deal. I didn't really want to go – Man City, even though a huge Club back then, were nothing like the footballing power that they are now, but the money was good, and I decided to give it a go.

I travelled over to train with Gary Megson, who still lived in Sheffield. 'Meggo' was always spot on with me – he had been a pro longer as he was older – his Dad, Don, was also a Wednesday legend, so he was a good counsel for a young lad and I always liked him and valued his advice. Some say he can be Marmite, but I have always had the highest regard for him.

Manchester City just did not work out, and for a wide variety of reasons. Mel Machin signed me, and we had some good lads there: Wayne Biggins was a Sheffield lad and they had Paul Lake, what a player he would have gone on to be had the injuries not got in the way. I would play with Brian Gayle at Sheffield United later, so plenty of characters.

I think I made seven or so appearances in the time I was there. I had gone from being in favor at one club to kicking my heels at another, and that was no good for me. Dave Bassett was doing great things at Sheffield United, and it really was a no brainer when he came in for me on loan at Bramall Lane. I didn't even have to think about it.

I knew many of the lads there anyway – especially people like Chris Wilder – and it was my Club. We eventually agreed a permanent deal, and I joined Sheffield United at a very special time. The club was a tight unit from the dressing rooms to the offices and out onto the pitch and into the terraces.

My parents had the Blue Bell pub on Main Street at Hackentorpe – a big Blades boozer, so there was never any place to hide if you had a bad game. It became a regular watering hole for the lads and we had some brilliant times. 'Harry' knew how to get the best out of players that no-one else seemed to want to touch or had a reputation. You cannot hide in Sheffield, if you went out then it was as a unit, and that could attract its own amount of bother. We stood together no matter what, and it would be fair to say that we got in a few scrapes, but all always backed each other up – that was the way it was for us.

The season ended with promotion, and the scenes at Leicester during and after were truly incredible. A great time to be a Blade and a player. Bear in mind that I started as a striker, then I got played as a winger before a spell in midfield. Later on, I became a wing back – it didn't matter to me where I played as long as I played – it was that simple.

Derek Dooley was Chief Executive at United, and we all loved him to bits. Even though he was old school he liked the laddish style that 'Harry' encouraged, and we had some laughs with Del, particularly on pre-season tours. He christened me, Dane Whitehouse and Mitch Ward 'The Slaps' for our antics, after the ice hockey team with a bad reputation in the Paul Newman file 'Slapshot', and the nickname stuck! Talk about give a dog a bad name!

My hardest time at the Lane was when I watched the FA Cup Semi-Final against the others from the stands at Wembley. I would have died to have played for United in that match in the same way that I would have died to play in any other, especially against them. Harry admitted later that his decision was a big mistake, and I agree with him. It needed as many of the Sheffield lads in that day who knew what it really meant. I got drunk to console myself, but it didn't dim the pain of not been able to go out and make a difference – to go and fight for the Club that I love. It still hurts today.

I have said that my older brother was also a bloody good football player – he represented, amongst others, Wednesday and Newcastle United, but my younger brother followed a completely different career path and became a hairdresser. It was whilst I was at United that he took the brave step of coming out and telling the world that he was gay. The climate was still different back then – it was no surprise to us, as we had long since worked things out. It made no difference to me – he is my brother, I love him and just want him to be happy and comfortable with himself and his life – it's that simple.

I went into the dressing room at the training ground and told everyone about his brave decision, adding that if anyone had an issue with it they were welcome to step outside and discuss it further – the lads all knew him, and all applauded his bravery – they knew it could not have been easy, and that sort of sums up what they all were to me and to each other. We were close, and it meant a lot.

I Captained the Club in the 1993/94 season, which for a local lad was a great honor. We began the age-old trick of selling our best players to balance the books, and it wasn't long before the board accepted a bid from Norwich City. I didn't want to leave, but the Club was a cracking one to join and the money on offer was so much more than I had ever earned at the Lane – I mean a King's ransom more.

We liked it there and it was a good side. Me and my wife had a young family by now, and we lived near the Broads – it was great. One night of stupidity ended that. I was involved in a fracas late one night with a taxi driver, and I was charged with assault. It's something I bitterly regret, and I feel they went out to make an example, but I ended up with a custodial sentence and my contract at Carrow Road being torn up for breach. I have had better times.

John Deehan, who I had worked with at Norwich, gave me a second chance at Wigan, and I had a great time at a Club that was on the up, and I was grateful for the chance. We reached the Division Two Play-offs and also lifted the Autoglass Shield at Wembley – good days at a cracking place. My League career ended with Scunthorpe after an altercation with manager Brian Laws, but that is another story for another time.

After playing Non-League, I set up my own building business – I had done a little bit with Lee Butler whilst still playing – we called it Bodgit and Scarper, honest we did! I am now as busy as I have ever been and really enjoy my work. My lad is doing really well in UK motorcross, which takes some time up. I also work most match days at Bramall Lane, hosting our sponsors and being around the commercial scene, which I also really enjoy – it's great to still play a part in things at the Club I love.

FOOTNOTE

I have known 'Bradders' for many years – we were at school together, and it would be harder to find a bigger character either on or off the field. As a player, he was hard and uncompromising and would have died for the shirt – it was as sim-

ple as that. As a Sheffield lad, he knew what it meant to do so, and never swerved the responsibility, not once. If ever a player fitted straight into the ethos of what Bassett was looking for, then it was Carl. The ability to work hard and play hard was there from the start, in that dressing room you needed strong characters, and he certainly fitted the bill. I would imagine there were plenty of sighs of relief in the Owls dressing room at Wembley in the semi when the teams were read out, wouldn't you? The journey across the city for any team is a huge one, but Carl did it without flinching. From a football point of view, he is always complimentary about his first employers and how he was treated by the Club and fans – he enjoyed his time there. As a Blade, he will stand his corner in any argument about the two. It's really that simple!